TEACHING TODAY
The Church's First Ministry

By
LOCKE E. BOWMAN, JR.

THE WESTMINSTER PRESS
Philadelphia

Scripture quotations from the Revised Standard Version of the Bible are copyrighted 1946, 1952, © 1971,
1973 by the Division of Christian Education of the
National Council of the Churches of Christ in the
U.S.A., and are used by permission.

BOOK DESIGN BY DOROTHY ALDEN SMITH

First edition

Published by The Westminster Press ®
Philadelphia, Pennsylvania

PRINTED IN THE UNITED STATES OF AMERICA

9 8 7 6 5 4 3 2 1

Library of Congress Cataloging in Publication Data

Bowman, Locke E
Teaching today.

Includes bibliographical references.
1. Christian education. I. Title.
BV1471.2.B66   268'.6   79-25901
ISBN 0-664-24303-7

This book is for my mother, Naomi,
who is in the 85th year of a life
that speaks of unwavering faith and goodness.

Contents

An Introduction

The Sunday school movement is two centuries old. Since I have been participant and observer in Sunday schools for more than twenty percent of those years, I believe I have acquired a bit of wisdom about this enduring vehicle of teaching/learning in the churches.

A lot of intemperate speaking and writing, mostly critical, has been directed at the Sunday school, and that is unfortunate. There is something utterly remarkable about this lay movement in the American churches, with its ability to attract lay volunteers as teachers, to offer special friendship and encouragement to children and youth, and to sustain weekly examination of Scripture and the issues of church and society.

In 1974, I published a little essay entitled "It's O.K. to Like Sunday School." It seems to have struck a responsive chord, for it was reprinted in national publications of the United Methodists, the Southern Baptists, the Nazarenes, and the Church of New Zealand. People still write to me about it. All I did was to make the case that good teaching could happen on Sunday quite as easily as Saturday, or Thursday evening, or any other time. The habit some people have of looking down their noses at Sunday school, or hurling the epithet, "That's Sunday school stuff!" to describe something intellectually inferior, is just plain unfair.

Defending Sunday school is hardly a dominant interest of mine, however. This book is about something more important than the specific local patterns the churches may perpetuate or devise anew. It will be a discussion about the nature of learning, the definition of teaching, and the essence of educating.

I have written with at least four audiences in mind: (1) persons interested in all aspects of education in our society, especially laypersons who care; (2) members of Christian churches who are also employed in public education as teachers or administrators; (3) volunteer teachers and professional educators in the parishes; and (4) clergy who are in decision-making roles about the direction of the churches in our time.

For the last fifteen years I have been peering intently at the "act of teaching." I find it the most engrossing sort of subject—sorely neglected among educationists who seem so often to observe from afar, noting only the broad strokes rather than the intriguing details of teacher-student encounter. I really believe that education, especially that accomplished by the church, will not be significantly improved or made lively on a wide scale, until more practitioners occupy themselves with the kinds of questions raised in this book—questions about how people learn, about the explicit functions of a teacher, and about the educative effect of Christian community. These are questions that prompt a task of reconstruction in which we all need to be engaged just now.

Teaching and learning can occur in Sunday school, and they do. But so can teaching and learning happen in many other church-related functions—formal and informal. The quality of what happens to individuals, as both learners and teachers, will not be determined by the settings alone. What matters most is the effort that proceeds from a well thought out vision on the part of people committed to "the ministry of teaching." I want to encourage that sense of vision.

Teaching as ministry, as service, is not confined to church. Christians who teach in public education are also engaged in *ministry,* although they may not employ that word to describe what they are doing.

Since World War II, the fortunes of educational effort in the churches and in the public schools have been somewhat similar, even intertwined. The churches opted for the vocabulary of general education when they started producing "curriculum" materials, and when they turned to educational specialists for assistance in shaping their views—pedagogues, psychologists, sociologists, and others.

As the printing presses started rolling in earnest in the late 1940's, the result was nothing like anything the Sunday school had ever seen before. It was a fascinating experience. The ferment of theology in the postwar years was combined with the best that could be gleaned from public education. The result was a heady mixture piled on the pages of textbooks, teacher's guides, manuals, packets, pamphlets, magazines, and more!

One day I looked at those mountains of published pieces and said to myself, "How on earth did Sunday school get so complicated?"

But it was understandable. Responsible bodies in the denominations were intent on trying to reach the masses with *insight,* with tools for interpretation, and with aids to improve family life, enhance social awareness, and bring about a just and durable peace.

The years from 1948 to 1973, a quarter of a century, were marked by incredibly creative and productive efforts on the part of Protestant denominations to come up with first-rate *materials* for teaching.

What is most remarkable indeed is that the sheer quantity of teaching materials made available to the parishes was matched by *quality.* Many of the best minds in the churches were recruited to write articles in church school curricula (note that "Sunday" was replaced by "church"; it was now "church school," or you weren't quite with it). Some future historian of the American churches will go through the files of all this curricular output and observe that all the right things were written, and at the right time.

We had a proliferation of well-organized curricular programs for education, arising out of the various theological and ecclesiastical traditions. Churches accepted these materials with surprising loyalty; some observers even worried about "orthopraxy" as a replacement for theological orthodoxy. Churches and pastors were judged by whether or not they used approved denominational curricular resources.

The curricula were all-embracing: they offered resources for teachers, clergy, parents, youth, and children, and they were attractively printed on the best kinds of paper.

Every major body of Protestants (Episcopal, Methodist, Presbyterian, Lutheran, Reformed, Congregational, Baptist, Disciples, and smaller groups as well) joined the move toward newer and better *materials*. The predictions in the early '60s were that the demand would increase for the rest of the century. Each "New Curriculum" was followed by the "new New . . . ."

Independent Protestant publishers (generally termed "nondenominational") improved the quality of their materials greatly. They had to, in order to keep up with the trend toward more and better.

By 1973, the last year in my selected quarter of a century, the Roman Catholic publishers were geared up to offer an enormous array of materials for the "new catechetics" (as a result of Vatican II). In many respects, the Catholic publishing scene is strikingly similar at this writing to the kind of effort undertaken by Protestants two decades or so earlier.

One interesting facet of the Protestant picture was that the "new" never fully supplanted the "old." The United Methodists' vast publishing enterprise offers a good example of how this was so. This denomination has a variety of

"new" curricular streams, all of them constantly undergo-
ing revision. But it still publishes the International Lesson
Series, with a history dating back for many decades—even
predating the old Federal Council of Churches. (At last
reading, the adult materials published by the United Methodists included 760,000 copies of *Adult Bible Studies,*
based on the international outlines.)

I referred to the optimism that prevailed in church education. It was like the optimism of public educators who
felt vindicated during the post-Sputnik years (dating from
1957); there would be a "new seriousness" in public
schools, to assure that only the best of everything would
suffice in any district. The culmination of this spurt of
curricular and pedagogical seriousness in public education
came in the early part of the Lyndon B. Johnson Administration; suddenly there was money for research and development, and a proliferation of innovative *materials*
flooded the market. "Innovation" was the big word.

For the churches, World War II was the event that prod-
ded Christian educators to work harder and produce
more. We felt a new urgency about teaching theological
truth and making sure that a world recovering from death,
suffering, and alienation would hear in clear terms the call
to Christian discipleship.

For the public schools, it was Sputnik—the challenge
from Soviet Russia, in the field of space exploration—that
produced a new sense of urgency. We would outteach and
more than match the Russians in technology; to stay ahead
meant pouring energy and resources into the educational
systems.

About the time of the first moon landing, in 1969, the
early signs of retrenchment began to occur in public education. We were engaged in a costly war in Southeast Asia
that was shortly to produce unparalleled unrest in American society. All was not well. Troubling questions about
every aspect of public education began to be raised; and
right now we are still in the throes of dealing with them

—with curricular organization, with structural and budge-
tary concerns, and with penetrating philosophical inquiry
into the nature of education itself. (I happen to believe
that public education, too, has failed to stress the fundamental issues of *how to teach* effectively.)

By 1970, the word "retrenchment" had taken on serious
overtones for the churches as well. National budgets were
dropping rapidly, so national staffs were being reduced.
Local church school attendance was declining from year
to year. The denominations began to take a hard look at
their independently conceived curricula. No longer were
they increasing in circulation. The whole enterprise of
"Christian education" began to crumble before our eyes.

Meanwhile, movements toward administrative restructuring that dated back to the late '50s had been progress-
ing slowly in most denominations—almost independently
from any of the educational considerations I have discussed above. The people involved in the structural questions throughout the churches were not thinking about
how to strengthen the teaching ministry of the parishes;
they were much more concerned with "regionalism" as
the wave of the future. They wanted to replace smaller
units of church administration with larger ones, to achieve
a streamlining and efficiency that seemed to be the logical
expected outcome of their planning. (Not once did it occur
to anyone that there would ever be less gasoline for travel
or that inflation would make travel budgets horrendous in
the enlarged regions!)

So there developed in the main-line Protestant denominations a curious mixture of factors:

1. Too much stress had been laid on curriculum *materials,* and not enough effort had been made to show people
how to *teach* effectively from them. The training events
related to church education were feeble when viewed
nationwide. Only a small percentage of the teachers in the
churches could actually use the materials with skill. Lo-
cally the parish programs suffered, and that more than any

other single factor *really precipitated the general decline.* What we needed was a lot of serious help in *how to teach* —in how to perceive and implement an effective ministry of teaching in the parishes. Pastors were at a loss to cope with this dilemma, for they were not skilled in the kinds of teaching the curricular materials demanded. They had few mental images of what to do to help lay teachers.

2. The denominations *had the answer* to the problem of training teachers, and the structures were there for disseminating it. In every small district of church administration were professionals and volunteers who were capable of getting close to the parishes and providing explicit, specific, helpful teacher training. Some of the "field" personnel of Christian education—and especially field representatives of the publishers—were able to do wonderfully creative things in workshops, laboratory classes, and the like. They needed only to *keep doing* and *expanding* what they were learning to do on a limited scale. We were very close to seeing that the curricular resources had to be accompanied by strong, energetic programs of training for local teachers if we were to have relevant, vital ministries of teaching. A real breakthrough *could* have happened, beginning around 1965.

3. But the answer so close by didn't stand a chance to be applied to the problems. Denominational restructuring had already gone too far. Administrative units were becoming larger and were assigned multiple areas of responsibility. The staff personnel for education, who had been most in touch with the parishes, were swept away in the process of change. Budgets were still declining on every hand, and preoccupation with structural issues sapped the energies of denominational leaders. Church education languished as a Protestant denominational concern; it became parochial all of a sudden.

And that is where we are now. The materials and structures are in a holding operation. Teacher training is still minimal. It is a time for rebuilding from the ground up.

In the '70s, the concept of Joint Educational Development came to fruition among several denominations. By then, the National Council of Churches (with its once-influential Division of Christian Education) was struggling to sustain its work in the face of decreased financial support. Some denominations felt keenly that cooperation must be strengthened, and they struggled valiantly to achieve methods of working together in order to salvage all that they could of educational ministry beyond the parish level. Among the results of their work (accomplished with the notable absence of all the Lutherans and of the United Methodists) was the cooperatively produced set of resources, *Christian Education: Shared Approaches.* Four streams of well-planned and helpful materials were made available to the churches from 1976 onward. The matter of teacher training had to be left largely to the local church structures.

What church teachers have needed most throughout the history of Christian education is guidance and encouragement in how to get from *materials* into the exciting act of *teaching.*

I do realize I have telescoped a great deal of history and have left out a lot of the other influential factors:

I have not discussed how the churches' involvement in the field of social action, especially in the era of the Vietnam war, impinged upon all that was happening to budgets, program, and the like.

Nor have I spoken of the pervasive influences of "secularization," greatly accelerated as a result of television, which has produced a great strain on families and parish life.

Nor have I written of the tragic, misguided "death of God" phenomenon as well as the breakdown of theological consensus, and the renewed vigor of evangelical conservatism.

I have not treated the special and separate case of Southern Baptist Sunday schools, in which evangelism is the most prominent emphasis.

I have not referred to the shifts in population groupings, and to the increase in numbers of working women, making for a reduced "pool" of capable volunteers with adequate time to give.

When you stop to think of how much we have gone through in the churches in the last fifteen years, it is no wonder so many people are weary to the bone. Our energies are sapped by the sheer effort to retain our sanity!

Yet for all my omissions and oversimplifications, I do believe I am right about the main points: We did not deal adequately, in main-line Protestantism, with *how to teach,* and we swept away the structures that offered the best possibility of helping in that task. We are, consequently, at a juncture where we have to start over, and I hope that we will start in the right place: with the concept of *teaching* as a primary ministry worthy of focused and unrelenting attention. Only that kind of new beginning will suffice.

So, this book is an effort to discuss anew the work of teachers. I hope that it will raise the consciousness of all four of my audiences, and that it will give heart to anyone who is willing to venture forth in the rebuilding that needs to happen. I am a person of hope—a Christian who has confidence. I believe we can envisage and bring to pass a genuine ministry of teaching in the future that will reach people in significant numbers with real depth of content. Perhaps, just perhaps, we can avoid some of the tactical errors of the past.

The outline for this book is based on three lectures I gave at the spring convocation of Eden Theological Seminary, Webster Groves, Missouri, in 1978. The good reception those lectures received emboldened me to expand them in this way.

I wish to acknowledge especially the generous assistance provided me in the days I was writing this volume:

the wonderfully supportive Board of Directors and staff of the National Teacher Education Project, for giving me study time; S. P. Reinertsen, for providing a home in California; Mrs. Louise Beck, librarian at San Francisco Theological Seminary, for many courtesies; and Mrs. James R. Scurlock, a truly gracious colleague and typist. Others not mentioned here will find themselves within the chapters that follow.

L.E.B., JR.

Scottsdale, Arizona

LEARNING / Act
of Creating

Behold, I make all things new.

Rev. 21:5

1 / Expanding Our Concepts of Learning

What does it mean to say, "I learned . . ."?

Everyone is a learner, but it is by no means obvious what we mean by the word "learning." I recall vividly a day when about eighty Christian educators became engaged in a heated and inconclusive debate over the difference between teaching and learning. Persons on one side of the room would offer an example of something said or done to promote teaching. Others would counter, seriously, that the proffered illustration was not so much "teaching" as "learning." Many of us left the room never to be the same again. We had experienced for ourselves an enduring dilemma: teaching and learning are inextricably intertwined. Were we teaching this to one another? Or were we learning it?

Augustine, in his dialogue *The Teacher,* written about A.D. 389, discusses with his son, Adeodatus, this same problem in logic:

Augustine: What would you say we are trying to do whenever we speak?

Adeodatus: As it strikes me right now, we want either to teach or to learn.

Augustine: I see, and I agree with one of these, but how does this hold for learning?

Adeodatus: How in the world do you suppose we learn, if not by asking questions?

Augustine: I think that even then we simply want to teach. Now I am inquiring of you whether you ask a question for any other reason than to teach the person asked what it is you want to know.[1]

As the dialogue continues, it is Augustine's position that teaching is calling something to the mind of another; but since, in recalling something to our own minds, there is the possibility of learning, we would have to conclude that this, too, is a form of teaching. There is a sense in which the learner is teaching himself or herself. Hence, learning is teaching—and teaching is learning. Still, we value the work of teachers, and we speak often of our having learned things.

What we conclude about the distinction between learning and teaching, in our own time, will rest inevitably on *how we view the nature of human beings.* How we think of ourselves, individually and in relation to others, will profoundly affect how we interpret the words, "I learned . . . ."

The most immediate context in which we are pressed to deal with this vital issue is the simmering controversy between behaviorism and humanism in current education. The very fact that many public and church school teachers alike can continue to function blithely without taking account of these polar positions is itself enough to underscore our need to raise questions anew about the nature of human beings, and of the acts of teaching and learning.

In its most extreme form, the behaviorist/humanist controversy centers on these true-false statements:

1. Human beings are functioning organisms, subject to forces from the *outside* that cause them to behave as they do.
2. Human beings are uniquely persons with *inner* potential, each one with a dynamic self-concept that results in individual patterns of growth.

Behaviorism

The first of these statements is the ultimate behavioral view of humanity. We are, of course, very complex beings, but the way in which we are shaped and conditioned is not all that different from what happens to other living beings, the behaviorist believes. It is unfair to accuse behaviorists of reducing people to animals (such as dogs and rats in experimental laboratories), for that was never their view or intention. Still, the emphasis in behaviorism is upon a fairly small number of explanatory concepts when discussing what is meant by learning:

We are, as organisms, subject to multiple stimuli. Certain responses to these stimuli are either reinforced or extinguished. The process is known as conditioning and counterconditioning. All learning is change in observable behaviors of the organism.

B. F. Skinner, whose name is immediately linked with behaviorism (a firm S-R connection, if there ever was one!) is a highly civilized person. He did not set out to diminish the status of humankind. But his investigations led him to the conclusion that people are "shaped" in their behavior by external contingencies. Given the time and inclination, we could analyze the causes of each person's behavior; to do so would involve retracing the intricate connections between the myriads of stimuli to which a person is subjected and the responses that were reinforced along the way.

The logical outcome of such a view, however, is to conclude that we are, in the end, lumps to be shaped. We are slates upon which outside forces write out the programs. Hence, *learning* is a matter of responding to what comes our way from outside ourselves. We are molded by something over which we do not have control.

Other thinkers who still regard themselves as primarily

behaviorists are less radical in their positions. They take instead a "social learning" view that recognizes a point at which the subjective self exerts controls. The learner gets to a stage where self-reinforcement occurs. But one must recognize that this modification of radical behaviorism still leaves the human being subject at the outset to external contingencies; it is only later that the subjective, inner factor begins to play a role.

Thus the issue becomes: Are we powerless in the final analysis? If so, then to learn is to fall under the power of something outside ourselves. If we are committed to the behaviorist's view, then the statement, "I learned . . . ," is an acknowledgment of submission as well as a fatal recognition of our sure limitations: we are responders.

It would be fairly easy to sweep aside behaviorism as irrelevant to the work of teaching/learning in the churches. But our actual practice, if honestly evaluated, reveals a behavioristic bent in Christian education. To be sure, few would call it by that name, yet here is the evidence:

Recitation of the "memory verse." This time-honored practice in Sunday school learning is a simple stimulus-response kind of function. The teacher says the verse and asks the students to repeat it. This process is reenacted several times until the stimulus ("Say today's memory verse") is followed by the appropriate response (the accurate recitation). Reinforcement occurs as the students are praised or otherwise rewarded. The behavior is maintained by continuing re-presentation of the stimulus.

Bible book "drills." (In an earlier day they were called "sword drills.") Students are asked to line up with Bibles held in a well-defined position (is it flat in the left hand?). The teacher calls out a Biblical reference by book, chapter, and verse (the S, stimulus). Students race against time to locate the passage and call out what they have found (the R, response). The teacher praises or gives tangible rewards. This behavior (being able to locate a Bible verse with speed and ease) is maintained through repetition of the drilling process.

Workbooks used in class. Lest someone say that memory verses and Bible drills are antiquated examples, hence not germane, we need look no farther than the array of current curricular resources published for use in church classes. Go through the student workbooks and notice all those blanks to be filled in, all those puzzles to be worked, all those mystery words to be discovered. What is the basis for developing and printing these? Students are being presented with a variety of stimuli designed to evoke certain responses. A blank to be filled in is the stimulus within a sentence-context. The student is to supply the appropriate response (the missing information or word). When the teacher checks the work done by the student, the reinforcement occurs (praise/reward). The resultant behavior is maintained through recitation: "Let's review what we have done in our workbooks."

The teacher who relies heavily on the workbook approach is aligned with the view that it is these external causes (blanks to be filled in, puzzles to be solved) that result in a student's being able to say, "I learned . . . ."

I daresay no teacher or learner is alive in the United States today who has not coped with some kind of workbook exercise. One year when I was a seventh-grader, every class I attended had a workbook to accompany it. From a course in civics I still recall filling in blanks that "taught" me the salary of the President (fixed at $75,000!) and the name of the Speaker of the House of Representatives (Bankhead—father of Tallulah, incidentally). The Secretary of State was Cordell Hull. What I supposedly "learned" from these clearly established S-R connections was a miscellany of facts soon to be outdated. Yet it vexes and troubles me as an educator that I still have them indelibly inscribed in my head. Is that a sure indication that S-R "works" and is therefore a necessary part of the teacher's repertoire? (Even that word "repertoire" comes out of the behaviorists' arsenal—what we have stored away in our S-R banks is our behavioral repertoire.)

My point is simply that none of us escapes what is essentially a behavioristic view of learning. It pops up at every turn of the way, and one might go so far as to say it appears every time a teacher assumes an authoritarian role. We shall note this repeatedly in succeeding chapters of this book.

Humanism

An alternative to behaviorism is a view of education termed "humanistic." The humanists' position is preoccupied with a focus on what is internal rather than external. Abraham Maslow and Carl Rogers are names inevitably associated with humanism. They emphasize the importance of subjective experiences, and they care about how persons see themselves. The "self-concept" is not something that stands still; it is constantly in flux, and it becomes the principle around which a person organizes experience.

The behaviorists can be quite articulate because they have less to talk about. I do not mean that to be a put-down; it is just that behaviorism is built around a limited number of concepts. In contrast, the humanists present a vast array of subtle commentary on the interaction between people and the environment. Maslow elaborates upon "self-actualization" as a process in which persons come to a positive realization of their potential. Rogers, whose influence has been widely felt in secular education, genuinely believes that every person is meant to pursue a direction called "growth." To the extent that people and institutions get in the way, a learner's growth is hampered or slowed. But if the right environmental conditions are present, learners can proceed full steam ahead. It is something inside, not outside, that produces the growth.[2]

According to Rogers, we have an inner nature that includes certain capacities, needs, talents, and natural balances that make for health and productivity. It is in the expression of this inner nature to its fullest that we experience ideal growth.

The key term for interpreting Rogers' view of teaching/learning is "positive regard." He distinguishes between the kind of positive regard that is conditional (in which children, for example, think of themselves as worthy only when they are doing what others expect of them) and the *un*conditional. In the unconditional situation, children are approved and respected for what they *are* rather than for the behaviors they exhibit. It is this fundamental respect for persons as individuals, each with unique characteristics, which makes possible the full expression of human beings' inner nature. Growth proceeds from being respected for what one *is* rather than for what one does by way of classroom performance. To say "I learned . . ." is, from the humanists' standpoint, a subjective declaration. We are speaking of personal movement over which we alone have control; it is always the learner who controls.

The humanists, therefore, are concerned about achievement of potential. They speak idealistically of learning as the act of finding out *how* to learn. Ultimately, one always looks inside the learner for clues that indicate paths of growth. It is this inside vs. outside issue that illuminates the behaviorist/humanist controversy.

Church education in recent years has been heavily affected by the humanistic approach to learning. We can cite these movements as evidence of it:

Stress on sensitivity. A spate of programs utilized in the secular sphere for helping persons to be sensitive to the views and feelings of others have found their way into Christian educators' practice. Sensitivity "training" in its various forms is the direct outgrowth of the humanistic emphasis. Training in active listening, in transactional analysis, in Rogerian "encounter" methods; use of the Magic Circle technique, or of est—all of these have appeared in the church classroom. So much depends on the thoroughness and skill of the leaders who introduce them. Some observers have noted that we all tend to opt for those programs which meet our own internal needs. If, for instance, we become aware that we are not the keen listeners we would like to be, we will prescribe "active listening" as a proper treatment for everyone.

Values clarification. Another "wave" from the humanists' side of the ledger is the emphasis on clarification of values through various exercises or strategies. The work of Louis Raths, popularized by Sidney Simon and others, has stressed the importance of our being able to affirm those things which we would be willing to declare as rock-bottom "values." These must be freely chosen and appropriated as our very own. We must be willing to state them in the presence of others and to act upon them consistently. Some highly creative efforts have occurred in churches where teachers have involved their students in affirming their religious values through the same kinds of strategies employed by the secular humanists.[3]

I came into the field of Christian education at a time when neo-orthodox theology seemed to rule out our use of the liberals' term "moral and spiritual values." So it has been interesting to see how, in the last few years, the word "values" has been reinstated to respectability. It has happened, I believe, in response to the humanistic trend in general education.

Open classrooms/education. The churches' interest in open classrooms, with learning centers and freedom of students to make choices regarding their own learning, is directly related to the humanistic influence. An emphasis on "individualized" learning stems from the viewpoint that each person grows at his or her own pace, in his or her own way. Open classrooms allow teachers to function as "facilitators" (Carl Rogers' term for teachers as helping persons). Churches have found this a congenial method, especially for combining various age levels in a classroom situation or for dealing with the frustrations of a totally voluntary attendance pattern.

Moral education. The identification of moral education as a specific field of interest among church educators is, it seems to me, another evidence of the humanistic influence. Recently, many church teachers have been interested in the practical application of Lawrence Kohlberg's "stages of moral development" to their own strategies with learners. The work of James Fowler and others falls into this same stream of influence.[4] As public educators have asked whether there are ways in which persons can be "moved" from one stage of moral development to another in the course of their classroom experience, church educators have followed suit. (I do not have time here to speak of the additional complicating factors of Freudian influences, Piagetian influences, and the like. I simply cite moral education as one more evidence of the humanist "side" that has its counterpart in church circles.)

The reader will note that these examples of humanistic influence are more general (less specific) than the ones given for behaviorism. Why is that the case? Because learners do not find it as easy (nor do teachers) to refer to specific "learnings" that occurred as a result of focusing upon the internal rather than the external.

Not long ago, I asked a group of one hundred thirty persons whether they could volunteer to share aloud some specific things they had learned within the preceding twelve months. Five people held up their hands; of the five, two were ministers who explained that they had learned such things as these: how to feel better about expressing themselves freely in a group; how to like people with whom they disagreed; how to lose weight and acquire greater self-esteem as a result. In each case, the respondents cited specific encounter groups (one led by a trainer in assertiveness, for instance) as the source of their new "learning."

Whatever else we may observe, there is something altogether different about these kinds of internalizing experiences. They are not the same as learning the books of the Bible, or mastering lists of moral injunctions, or acquiring other "data."

Having cast this discussion in the context of the behaviorist/humanist controversy, we must ask whether there is any way out of the seeming impasse. The two sides take such centrally opposing views of the *nature of humankind* that one wonders whether there is any possibility of reconciliation between them.

Three approaches to the problem are often tried:

1. We may say that behaviorism and humanism are simply complementary. For some types of learning, we need to recognize the S-R model as valid; but for certain aspects of human growth, S-R doesn't "work," so we acknowledge that other factors are operative. (It is appropriate, therefore, to insist on the Bible book drills so that students will "get" this necessary information, useful for a lifetime. But when it comes to helping persons to express love toward others, entirely different and more subtle strategies are involved. We use *both* approaches.)

2. Humanism can be "boiled down" to behaviorism. This approach suggests that when a teacher and learner are professing to be freely relating to each other and dealing with highly subjective material, they are in fact utilizing the S-R model; it is simply at a level of greater sophistication. The "facilitating teacher" is making subtle use of reinforcement technique; without realizing it, the parties to the process are actually engaged in the behavioristic patterns of procedure.

3. Behaviorism can be "boiled down" to humanism. Advocates of this approach contend that S-R is effective only when the teacher is perceived as a caring, concerned individual. In those instances where teachers are professing to be behavioristically oriented, they are in fact showing unconditional positive regard for their students throughout the day. And it is this human fac-

tor which simply makes S-R appear to be effective![5]

None of these three efforts at reconciliation seems satisfactory, and especially not to the church education scene. We are clearly in need of some other way of speaking about learning that will help us find our way. Is there a way of saying "I learned . . ." that allows us to bring into play our views as Christians?

Learning as Creating

Our best hope of having something distinctive to contribute to an understanding of learning is to be found in the Christian understanding of creation. We are created beings, made in the image of God and given a role to fulfill in God's continuing purpose for the whole of creation.[6] As creatures of God, we are free to be creative ourselves. I have come more and more to look upon all learning as an act of creating, and the remainder of this book will be devoted to that theme.

Neither the behaviorists, with their extensive influence over all education, nor the radical humanists, with their widespread influence within the church as well as the secular sphere, have very much to say about God. Religious notions are regarded as cultural phenomena, possibly convenient for those who get involved with that sort of thing—but serious interest in theological affirmations about people's lives is wanting in both houses.

Christians live and work in a culture that is at best confused about the meaning and importance of faith in God as Creator. In such a culture we are called upon to teach and learn, and we cannot divorce ourselves from the language, the jargon, of the vast educational enterprise. Unless we choose to withdraw from the mainstream of society, electing not to take part in the debates and evaluations regarding educational purpose and method, we need to get our thinking organized for making a singular contribution. There is a way, I do believe, for us to make sense out of the words, "I learned . . . ," without yielding to the key suppositions about humankind that govern behaviorism and humanism.

Sometimes we shall do and say things that look and sound very much like humanistic education. But we shall be using similar words and phrases, similar techniques and resources, with our own theological presuppositions governing our usage. We need not retreat into our own corner; indeed, I should like to think we could offer new light to the whole enterprise of education in our time.

Let us begin by considering what it means to think of ourselves as God's created people. We are made "in the image" of God, having qualities of mind and heart that are divinely bestowed. We are unique among all creatures, and we are responsible to the Creator.

Study a Biblical concordance, with a view to comparing the usages of the words "create," "make," and "build." English translators have usually reserved the word "create" for the work of God, in fashioning and forming the universe and all the creatures in it. But notice how many times "make" and "build" are used to describe the work of humankind as well as God. Under God, we are makers and builders. The Scriptures are not a textbook on anthropology or psychology, or education. But they present a picture of God's people as making and building, exercising lavishly their own intelligence and gifts.

Sometimes the results of human making are contrary to the will and purpose of God. In the case of the tower of Babel (Gen., ch. 11), the building is a genuine misuse of humankind's capacity for putting things together—for making! The result is divine judgment—a confounding of a misguided human project. The builders sinned in usurping their Creator's role; they overstepped the limits placed upon human effort.

We are led to speak, then, of human creativity as a creativity exercised in humble supplication that what we create will be acceptable to *the* Creator. There is simply no way to avoid using the word "creative" for the work of people. But in doing so, we affirm: All that we build, all that we make, is subject to God's evaluation. God uses our hands to accomplish purposes that only God can work out. Christians profess that God is making all things "new," that in Christ a new work of creation has begun and is continuing. Christians see themselves as participants in that work.

It is on such a foundation that we must lay our learning theory. When we speak of learning, we are speaking of creation—of acts that can best be described as making and building.

Several times, recently, when I have spoken about people as creators, I have been heartily challenged by laypersons who will say: "But only God creates! We are not creators of anything at all." This elicits, of course, the centuries-old discussion about *creatio ex nihilo* (that only God creates, since God alone is capable of making something from nothing—truly "from the beginning" when there was only the divine Mind, Word, Cause). For some persons it appears to be impossible to speak of human beings as creators, since we are incapable of *creatio ex nihilo*. Since we can only make something out of something, this is not really creating.

This sort of discussion is a dead end, and it is not even consistent with the Genesis account. God creates people out of dust—out of something *(substantia)*. Hence, God's own making of things cannot always be described as *creatio ex nihilo*. The continuing work of creating is from something to something. And in that sense, as participants in the realm of creation, made in the image of God the Creator, *we* create (make, build) all the time!

God-given Creativity

Human creativity is a God-given reality. The products of human genius, imagination, and inventiveness are everywhere around us. The facets of civilization—language, art, science, economics, and government—are the results of human creativity. All are subject, indeed, to divine judgment; but all are the direct consequence of freedom exercised under God.

So I have no trouble at all with speaking of human beings as creators. I believe we are creating when we are truly learning. To say "I learned . . ." is to say "I have created . . . ."

How is it that learning is an act of creating? And what sets such a statement apart from the current behavioristic and humanistic trends in education?

First, we must consider what is involved in creating (making, building):

1. *An act of the will.* Whether consciously or unconsciously, the creator decides to do something. "I will make," or "I will build," or "I will try, and we'll see what happens," or "I will experiment." These are the beginnings of the creative act. We decide to be active, we take the initiative, we make some sort of move in a direction.

2. *Something to work with.* As we have seen, our creativity depends upon our utilization of materials, ideas, and combinations of substance that are already at hand. We manipulate, arrange, and form the products of our hands, minds, and hearts, but we can only work from what we had to start with. (It is right along here that the behaviorists remind us of the need for a "repertoire" to draw upon.)

3. *Ability to evaluate.* Once we have completed a creative act, we are able to look back upon it and form a judgment about it. When God created, the work was pronounced "good." As we function in God's image, we are able to say the same of our own work, or to criticize it, or to reject it and destroy it. We decide whether our creations shall be permitted to continue; preservation and conservation of our achievements are within our power to grant or withhold.

An *act of learning* involves all three of these elements. When a person says, "I learned . . . ," he or she is speaking about having performed an act of the will, having utilized something in order to make a new something uniquely his or her own, and having decided what to do with the product (evaluated it). Anything worthy of being called learning will, I believe, exhibit this sort of movement. It will *not*, however, be a neat one-two-three procedure. The willing, the taking of initiative, is not always a conscious activity undertaken at a time set aside for "being creative." Seldom does one have the capacity to undertake creative endeavors on a "schedule." We are sometimes aware that creativity has occurred somewhat below the surface of our consciousness.

Mortimer Adler speaks of times when he has faced what seemed to be obstacles to the creative solution of a problem. He has put the problem aside, pronouncing it insoluble, only to be overtaken at a later moment with a flash of insight that brought the long-sought answer. The creative act, the learning, didn't happen on schedule; a kind of inner chaos was sorted out in a way that defies precise description. We have all had that kind of experience when "sleeping" on a problem. The "something to work with" was not consciously present; it came to us "in the night" or "out of the blue" or "by surprise," we say.

But this intuitive, often mysterious aspect of creativity —of learning— does not negate the essentials I have outlined. Surely this is related to the importance of visions and dreams in the Biblical accounts. Peter learns—that is, he creates—a new image of the gospel's impact for non-Jews, in response to a vision (Acts, ch. 10). The universality of Christ's redeeming work is learned, created afresh, in the mind of the apostle; it is preserved as a guiding principle in the church from that day on. God is the Author of this human creating, to be sure. But as teachers and learners we have a duty to search for understanding and to ask, How do people learn things? They learn, it seems to me, by willing and evaluating—and always in relation to the media (the *substantia*)[7] that are available to them: ideas, materials, and infinite possibilities for combinations of substance.

We are created with the capacity to initiate—and to the extent that we do so, we learn. In taking initiative, in making moves that lead to something (for us), we produce the kind of result that causes us to say, "I learned . . . ." It is surely an act of creating.

In an earlier day it was common for some theologians to speak of the extra-Biblical idea of "the divine spark" that was present in the Creation, to give to human beings a character unlike any other species. We no longer speak of such a spark as the distinguishing mark of personhood. But in a sense it is usefully suggestive in a discussion about what happens in the act of learning, especially when we contrast a dynamic view of persons with the behavioristic tendency to think of learners as malleable. One may subject a person to countless S-R transactions, carefully sequenced and designed to produce a given outcome or objective. But unless there is some sort of "spark" in the process, the elements of creativity are missing. No active willing to produce something for oneself or others is ignited.

The humanists sense this "spark" phenomenon keenly, and so they speak of the inner drives that must be released —of growth that must be promoted through the "liberating" of the self to achieve its natural potential (note the use of "natural," without allusion to God as Creator).

A theory of learning based on Creation and creating, seen from a Christian perspective, is not so optimistic about human potential for good as the humanist is required to be. The humanistic view of education and learning places its articles of faith in the human being. To the extent that God plays a role in such a view, it is at the will of humankind; ultimately, God is the creation of human beings—a culturally produced God cast in the image of persons. Thus the humanist is fully in charge of human destiny; in the long run, there is no choice but optimism. Things will turn out all right in the end.

Behaviorists tend to avoid such matters in discussion and practice. What matters most to them is survival and the perpetuation of what is known. Hope is rooted in rational achievement through meticulous investigation and explanation at an empirical level rather than through spiritual insight or philosophic or aesthetic inspiration.

Potential for Good or Evil

When Christians ponder the behaviorism/humanism issue, they come at it from a unique stance in regard to human nature; it is informed by a theological view.

We are aware of the possibilities for nobility in human souls, but we know all persons sin and fall short. It comes as no surprise to us when human ventures turn out badly —the human scene is a mixture of good and evil, of sin and redemption, of covenant obedience and woeful straying from the will of God. Such healthy realism is no cause for despair, for we know the battle to be won in Christ who is at work to "make all things new." But the fullness of time has not yet come; we work in faith and in appropriate humility. We are not in charge—God is. And that sort of "captivity" under God is paradoxically the most liberating kind of idea we can encounter. We are free to be God's learners—his collaborating creators in this age! That is a good expression, "collaborating creators." We co-labor with the Creator, aware of the promise that, in Christ, all things shall be made new. To the extent we do so, we learn (make, build) for ourselves and others.

I intend to dwell upon such a view of learning and to show how it can affect our ministry of teaching. It has a lot to do with the fact that "I learned . . ." is a much more significant statement than "I remember . . . ."

The behaviorally oriented teacher/educator is preoc-

cupied with producing indelible markings within the
human memory. Consider any instance of programmed
instruction, or the use of teaching machines or computer-
aided systems of instruction. So much depends on remembering things in the right order and recalling them when
asked. If the memory fails, it is because the reinforcement
was inadequte. If undesired behaviors persist (are remembered and acted out), then extinction must be the order of
the day; provision is made for extinguishing things from
learners' repertoire.

In all honesty, there must be something to this! How else
can we account for the myriads of things we all have in our
heads that seem to have gotten there through patterns of
repetition? Now that they are stored, they will not seem
to go away. For instance, here's 253-W, the telephone
number of a dear friend of 1943. Telephones in those days,
especially in small towns like the one where I lived, didn't
have the modern seven-digit numbers we all take for
granted. The friend is long dead; the phone system is fully
modernized, and no one anywhere has such a number.
Around 1945, there was a Greyhound commuter bus in
Kansas City that had that same number, 253-W, and every
time I would ride that bus, I would think of my friend.
Reinforced, reinforced, never extinguished, 253-W is
there until I die, I suppose. It is something I *remember*.
But does that have anything at all to do with what we can
truly call learning? I don't think so. It is a psycho-bio-
mechanical something that is part of my storehouse—a
sort of *mental debris*. Such debris abounds in somewhat
the same way that other sorts of debris gather in any system that functions twenty-four hours a day, year after
year. Of all such material, we can say "I remember . . . ,"
but it is not essentially related to learning.

Still another example will help to contrast mere remembering with real learning. For some years now I have been
working crossword puzzles, and I have finally graduated
to the *New York Times* puzzles, which are far more chal-

lenging and interesting to do. Here is a puzzle that asks for "African antelope." I remember that it is "eland." A "bitter vetch" is "ers," and a "maple genus" is "acer." These are all simply words that I remember from having used them over and over. They have been reinforced in some way, so that they are part of my mental collection of attic pieces; I can go to the attic and get them when they will serve a useful "across" or "down" purpose in a puzzle which I do for sheer pleasure. This sort of operation has very little to do with learning; it is simply a psycho-bio-mechanical undertaking.

Then one day I am working a puzzle, and it calls for a French artist's name. The first letter is "M," and it has five letters. It must be Manet, but that won't work. I conclude that it is Monet. Now I am arrested by this little episode. I cannot recall ever having considered which of these preceded the other one—or were they contemporaries? I have to find out; I am not satisfied to remain unaware, unenlightened. I go to the encyclopedia, and before long I am absorbed in reading about expressionism and impressionism in art. I am able to find out where Manet and Monet fit into the scheme of art history. Just consider what happened to me: I made a deliberate move in a direction (I willed to use the encyclopedia). I used what I had (ability to read, to find things, to understand what I was reading), and I built something that had not been there before, for me. It felt rewarding, and I can evaluate that experience as positive.

The puzzle—a strict behaviorist would call it a "stimulus" that produced a complex activity as a "response."

The puzzle—a strict humanist would call it a subjective pleasure that aroused an inner drive "to know."

The puzzle—I think of it as a simple human activity that is sometimes (not often, for me) capable of inducing a creative act.

Whatever one concludes about it, you have to say that there is a difference between automatically penciling in "ers" as a bitter vetch and pondering thoughtfully the lives of Manet and Monet, the French artists! The one activity relates only to "I remember . . . ." The other clearly relates also to "I learned . . . ."

If we are going to make sense out of teaching and learning, learning and teaching, we have to spend some time pondering just such fascinating distinctions. I shall try in succeeding chapters to be consistent with the view I have laid out here: Learning is an act of creating. And when I say "creating," I am thinking of it as collaboration with God the Creator—source of all that is or will be. It is participating in the work of Christ who makes "all things new."

2 / Acquiring Insights Creatively

Many persons in general education as well as church education today think of learners as ideally passive. How many times have you heard a teacher say of a church school class: "They're becoming a good group. They sit and listen quite well"? Listening can be a very positive thing, especially in the presence of a good storyteller. But listless receptivity, on students' part, to whatever a teacher does to them is hardly an appropriate model for the kind of approach to learning I was sketching in the preceding chapter.

Both the behaviorists and the humanists would opt for active students—the former in order to assure evidence of the S-R connections, the latter in order to affirm that growth is occurring.

Likewise, if we are to think of learning as creating, the implication is clear that the learner is active—mentally, physically, emotionally, totally active. It is the hope of effective teachers that this active role will be cultivated on the part of everyone involved in education, including the teacher.

In fact, the stress upon the words "action" and "active" has been present in discussions of teaching/learning for as long as education has been a subject of investigation. In his famous essay, "The Aims of Education," Alfred North Whitehead spoke of "activity of thought" as synonymous with culture. It is the aim of teachers and learners to make use of ideas. Whitehead disdained what he called "inert ideas" ("received into the mind without being utilised, or tested, or thrown into fresh combinations").[8]

To guard against seeding the mind with countless disconnected ideas that are inert ("mental dryrot," he called it), Whitehead suggested two "educational commandments":

"Do not teach too many subjects."

"What you teach, teach thoroughly."

If Whitehead could see the results of some of our behaviorally oriented curricula, preoccupied with minutiae, he would surely ask: What prevents all this from becoming inert? Where is the activity of thought?

I find a singular correspondence between Whitehead's commandments and my own emphasis in the last ten years upon the importance of "main ideas," or "key concepts," in our teaching and learning. Indeed, Whitehead himself says: "Let the main ideas which are introduced into a child's education be few and important, and let them be thrown into every combination possible. The child should make them his own, and should understand their application here and now in the circumstances of his actual life."

Notice how Whitehead uses the expression, twice quoted above, "thrown into . . . combinations." It is the job of a learner—and nothing else can really be called true learning—to play around with ideas, to work with everything at hand in his or her mind in order to create something, or to make something that is fresh and new for him or her.

If, for instance, I introduce to a group of students the concept of covenant (the main idea of forming a binding agreement between a people and their God), then it is my duty as teacher/learner to involve students in pursuing that concept to the fullest. How did covenant-making get started? Who makes covenants? And where does covenant-making lead? Such a study could become a motif for a long, long period of investigation and discovery, and it would attract to itself (as it does in certain theologies) the related concepts of faith, trust, sin, and obedience, and on and on. It is an act of creating for every learner to build an individual and relevant concept of covenant.

To me that makes sound sense, and it can be a most exciting enterprise. I find it baffling, incidentally, that curriculum builders have for the most part studiously avoided such thoroughness in the preparation of study materials. Curricula continue to disobey religiously the Whitehead commandment, "Do not teach too many subjects." The result is a tendency to write sprinklings of information about dozens of ideas destined to become "inert." We shall return to this later.

For now, it is essential to note that when I speak of "creating," I am not thinking of something that is new for the human race. It is instead an act of making something that was not there before *for the individual.* The newness is for the creator.

A preschool teacher gathers up the wet finger-painting sheets and hangs them on the line to dry. Each one has the identifying marks of an individual child. It is tempting for the teacher, who has been working at this job for several years, to think: Well, one more day of finger painting. They all look just alike from year to year! But it is not so for each young person. Every one of those sheets on the line is potentially a creation, an act of learning. To use Whitehead's phrases, it is possible that a child, in making a finger painting, was consciously throwing something into a "fresh combination"—and it is that "activity of thought" we call learning. The similarities in the products of the preschoolers is beside the point; the uniqueness of each one is what counts.

We all engage in continuous replication of the experience of humankind. (I am doing that in the writing of this book.) But each of us also performs uniquely in the formation of our interior patterns of thinking and being.

It should be no surprise to teachers, therefore, that their students frequently learn something quite different from what the teachers intended them to accomplish through a lesson or activity. The creators are all at work, each in a singular path of pursuit, and the results are never uniform or totally predictable.

Some Things I Learned and How

Ultimately, only a learner can speak authentically about what has been learned and how. Neither teachers nor anyone else can ever fully enter into the experience of another. For that reason, I will share several examples of things I have learned. For the last few years I have spoken about these with other teachers in the church, in order to stir their own memories and elicit parallel experiences that could be discussed as illustrative of the act of learning as creative. As the reader follows, let that same process occur here: Think of your own pilgrimage, asking yourself, When has something like this happened to *me?*

Physical principle with implications. On an autumn day in the ninth-grade science class, our teacher took a small group of us outdoors to his automobile. He raised the hood and pointed to the positive and negative poles of the battery. A plus sign indicated positive, a minus sign indicated negative. He used a piece of metal to show what would happen if these positive and negative poles were touched simultaneously—sparks were caused!

Something happened for me, and it had nothing to do with motors' functioning (the main topic of that day's class). I put some things together in a new combination.

I had learned about plus and minus signs in grade 1. They were simply indicators of what I was expected to do with pairs of figures—to add or to subtract. (Believe it or not, mathematical instruction in my childhood was confined largely to operations we were told to perform, and I had no concept of a numbers line with zero in the middle and the positive integers to the right, the negative integers to the left. It didn't come clear to me even in my study of algebra. Not until I was an adult did I learn about the positive and negative numbers proceeding infinitely in opposite directions.)

But now, as I looked at that battery and thought about those opposites, "positive" and "negative," a whole new world opened up for me. I would never be the same. I lay awake in my bed that night, marveling at how the whole world seemed filled with positive and negative types of spark-producing attractions. I thought: Heaven is positive; hell is negative. Up is more positive than negative; down is more negative than positive. For our family, Democrat was positive and Republican was negative. At a street intersection, green is positive and red is negative.

I had learned something—I had created my own special road of inquiry based on plus and minus, which I brought to school with me that day, and I had begun to integrate the new evidence (physically demonstrated by a teacher) that these signs could be linked with positive and negative interaction. I have no idea whether anyone else in that small group of students was so affected, but for me it was a remarkable opportunity for creative reflection . . . and I have never discarded it. I am still creating from that discovery of a universal principle.

Linking of fantasy with reality. I believe I can recall the first time I made a conscious connection between something fantasized and its counterpart in reality.

My father had talked with me during my childhood (which coincided with the years of the Great Depression) about the wonders of the three-ring circus. I could only consider in sheer fantasy what it must be like.

Then the Barnum and Bailey Circus came to town (in the days before it had combined with Ringling Brothers). Circus day was Sunday, and this posed something of a problem for my father. He strongly disapproved of a circus performance on Sunday, but he could not bear to deprive his son of the chance to see such a wonderful thing. So we went. It was one of the happiest days of my life, and I reveled in it. I was lost in it for days afterward, walking about as if in a dream.

Then, when I began to enter the real world again, I found a cable to stretch between two trees. With sticks for a balance, I tried to walk the wire myself, as I had seen it done. I had a small trapeze on a tree limb, and I learned to do more with it than I dreamed I could. A few neighbor children and my grandfather became the audience for my very own circus performance. I was able to combine fantasy with an extraordinary personal experience that approximated it, and then to add an element of personal practice. The circus became mine, in reality, and it still belongs to me. I learned "circus," and for me it was an act of *making* circus in a movement from fantasy to the real thing.

I am quite certain that children sometimes move today from the fantasy world of television into creative efforts to reproduce these experiences for themselves, to the degree they are able. In 1979, we read of a four-year-old boy who attempted to fly from a window in the way a super-being he had watched on television had done it. Within hours he died from his injuries.

And it seems to me that one reason for the persistence of pornography in the fields of graphic arts and cinema is partly related to the human proclivity for acting out fantasy. It is a form of learning that cannot be ignored. Our sexuality, however intensely private and personal, is not truly possessed until explored and made ours in creative acts of learning. The phenomenon of filmed pornography is at least understandable, if not forgivable, when seen as an instance of our seeking to move from private fantasy to observed and possibly relevant experiences. The camera provides more than we produce in our own imagination.

Liturgy and spirituality. Of all the things that have happened to me in the church, the most constructive experience has been learning more about prayer. I cannot remember when I was not able in some fashion to address my deepest thoughts to God. But I used to wonder, as a child and especially as a teen-ager: Is there some sort of guidance in how to pray? Some sort of principle to bring more order into the act of praying? I disliked the idea that my own prayers would always be a jumble, formless or in disarray.

It was not until I was a student in theological seminary that I learned about adoration, confession, thanksgiving, supplication, and intercession. A kind teacher supplied these names for types of praying and helped me to identify examples of each. My personal praying began to be so much more satisfying as I entered a whole world of liturgical spirituality that had been alien to my youth. (To be sure, I had been exposed to those elements of prayer over and over, but I was never made conscious of them in such a way as to be able to make them my own.)

A personal need caused me to combine what I knew and felt with what was readily available in liturgy, and thus I was able to create for myself something that was not new at all for the church, but surely quite new and deeply meaningful to me. I learned to pray.

So much for personal examples. These three are enough to illustrate how learning as an act of creating is a constant possibility in home and family, routines of daily living, school and academics, church and liturgy, and the larger world. Each example shows the learner taking some initiative, and unavoidably so, as a creator.

Learning often happens in structured settings, in quite academic surroundings. We should hope so, since we spend so much money and time in the confidence that learning will occur in institutions established for that purpose. But sometimes learning happens in quite serendipitous moments.

Regardless of *where* the learning begins or leads, it has to be a creative act that uses the stuff of reality in moments when meaning can invade it—for us, where *we* are!

I love Fynn's marvelous true story of a little Cockney girl who inspired *Mister God, This Is Anna.*[9] Her most productive seasons of learning occurred in everyday experiences on London streets. She constructed highly sophisticated philosophical and mathematical principles that revealed her to be an unmistakable genius.

Anna could expound on infinity, but she couldn't abide a story problem that required her to multiply three straight rows in a garden by twenty flowers each. If you planted flowers that way, you "shouldn't have no bloody flowers!" she fulminated. Sure enough. Why make into an inert idea something so exciting as mathematical quantity? Great ideas deserve to be put together into new and wonderful combinations, and Anna sensed this intuitively; the story problems were a disservice to her and to mathematics as well.

Moments of Learning

After a dozen years in which I have observed many hundreds of hours of teaching episodes, I am grateful for the recollection of times when students and teachers exhibited *activity of thought* worthy of God's creative people.

Many other teachers who read this chapter will be able to supply examples fully as interesting as these:

1. *How it really was.* The curriculum book for grades 3–4 in a laboratory class included a lesson on Abraham's near-sacrifice of his son, Isaac. The story had been reconstructed by the writer so that the knife was left out, and the terror was at least diminished if not blunted altogether. The teacher used the story just as it appeared in the book, with a group of interested youngsters gathered comfortably on the rug to listen.

The last phrase concluded, the teacher put down the

book and made a move to involve the students in the next activity on the lesson plan.

"That's not the way it really was!" Billy, a serious-minded third-grader spoke matter-of-factly but also insistently. "Abraham had a knife in his hand, and he was about to stick it into Isaac's neck, just the way you'd kill a sheep," he said.

The teacher started to speak, noting the keen interest of all the other class members. But Billy had not finished. "Here, I can find that story in my Bible!" He turned with skill to the right spot in Genesis, ch. 22, and he started reading aloud how Abraham had come so close to killing his precious son, Isaac.

What was there to do? The atmosphere in the classroom was electric. The curriculum's watered-down version of the story had clearly been unacceptable.

Something remarkable happened, in my opinion. The teacher wisely spoke of the puzzling story in relation to the practice of child sacrifice in cultures Abraham would have known about. The children in that class were able, in that instance, to grasp the likely reason for the episode in Abraham's life. God did not require of Abraham that he follow suit and sacrifice his child as others did, who did not know the one true God. It made sense that Abraham would be submitted to such a test, and that the outcome would be a vivid demonstration of the unique character of our God in contrast to alien gods.

I cannot say for sure, but I trust my hunch that, for Billy at least, the frank and honest response by the teacher to his own call for a valid rendering of the text, led to something creative and new for him. He had the story down cold, and he knew where to find it. But he needed to share in the questions: Why is this story here? What is its probable meaning?

Yes, sometimes third- and fourth-graders are able to engage in interpretive skills, just as they did in this class.

In our haste to protect children from the harsher details of some of the Biblical accounts, we may be depriving them of just the furnishings of mind they need in order to sense the Scriptures' way of speaking directly to life as it really is.

I hasten to add that we can go too far in the opposite direction, overdramatizing the stories in such a way that we emphasize the details more than the story line. I saw that happen once with a young, inexperienced teacher who decided to do a dramatic reenactment of the Abraham-Isaac story, complete with knife! It was a disaster; the children in his class, especially the boy chosen to play Isaac, were simply unable to cope with such a portrayal.

2. *He'd care about the other side of town.* I suppose I have observed a score of teaching sessions, for children, youth, or adults, that focused on the prophet Amos. This prophet of justice, who spoke to Israel and Judah alike, can be studied thoroughly—and his message is relevant to each time and place.

Students may take a direct approach, seeking to understand the prophecy and its background, line by line. Or they may work inductively, examining evidence of injustice in the world and then listening to what the man Amos has to say in a situation not wholly dissimilar.

I recall in particular an afternoon when a group of students in grades 5–6 were involved in a variety of learning activities related to Amos. A tape recording that provided the historical background of the prophecy had been prepared, and students had listened in a learning center. Pictures contrasting justice and injustice were examined and discussed in small groups. Another small-group exercise involved reading selected passages from Amos and discussing together questions related to the theme of *justice* that shall "run down as waters" (Amos 5:24).

Then the teacher put on the chalkboard the statement, "If Amos came to this town [where the class was being held], he wouldn't have much to say." Students were asked to indicate whether they agreed or disagreed with the statement. Most of them disagreed, and the teacher asked why. They were not especially responsive.

In a quiet moment, the teacher probed once more. "If the prophet Amos, the man we have studied today, were to come to this town, what do you think he might say to the people here—or to us?"

There was a long pause, and then something wonderful happened. A sixth-grader raised her hand tentatively. The teacher nodded to her, and she spoke: "We are having a bond election here to decide whether the people will pay for a new park system. But the parks, if the money comes for them, will all be on one side of town where the people with the nicest homes live. I think this isn't fair to the poor people on the other side. And if Amos were here, he would say something about that!"

The moment every teacher hopes for—when students will move from the abstract to the real, the concrete—had arrived in this class. The group could identify with what their classmate had said. Something creative had begun, and a new point of view that included an Old Testament figure as well as the students' contemporaries was now being constructed. Although I cannot know for certain, I have an intuitive feeling that something called learning was taking place for these boys and girls. Active thought brought ideas into new combinations.

3. *Oh, it's not that bad.* One unforgettable laboratory session involved a class for students in grades 7–8. This time, the study had included an examination of the prophet Elijah.

Students had been given curriculum books that were quite well prepared; it was their job to ferret out the key facts about the prophet's life. The articles they read referred to cited Bible references, and the students worked diligently at looking up these lines and taking note of the details.

184020

After this period of research, the teachers in a teaching team called on the students to report what they had found out. Taking turns, the boys and girls did an excellent job of making Elijah's story come to life.

In fact, the contest between Elijah and the prophets of Baal, in which Elijah's supplications brought down fire upon the altar, was especially interesting to the junior highs. They told it with gusto. And they included the destruction of the false prophets in their account, of course.

One of the teachers, somewhat prone to feel squeamish about Old Testament stories, exclaimed: "Isn't that terrible? Think of those four hundred men who lost their lives. I'm not sure I can feel very good about that sort of story."

One of the class members was a more mature boy who spoke in a deep voice: "Oh, that's not so bad. Our country lost more than one hundred times that many men in the Vietnam war, and that was just a small war."

Again, it was one of those insightful moments in a classroom where an observer senses an "electric" reaction. Teacher and students together faced honestly their feelings about the "relative" value of human life. Why do we recoil from historical accounts of multiple deaths but manage to handle almost routinely the daily loss of life in international and civil conflicts, or in automobile accidents, or as a result of crime and other violence?

I am virtually certain that both the teacher and the students in that class experienced together a creative encounter leading to the construction of something new for them, something that was not there before. Learning had taken place.

4. *When was his name changed?* This last example, involving a men's Bible class, comes out of my own pastoral experience. Because it is so much like what I have seen happening many times over in church studies, I believe it useful to add here.

For several weeks I had been teaching the group, and we were reviewing the history of the people of God in the

Old Testament. On this particular Sunday I had given what I felt was an unusually good presentation on the period of Saul, the king. I described his relationship to young David, and I left no bit of data untouched. It was a satisfying sort of feeling to conclude the lesson and to ask, "Are there questions you may have?" By my watch, there were possibly ten or twelve minutes left in the class period.

A member of the class was a mail carrier, a dear friend to me throughout my pastorate. He had attended the church all his life, and he had been a member of Sunday school classes there ever since he was a small boy.

It was this friend who asked the question that morning. He said, "Now when did his [Saul's] name get changed to Paul?"

In that instant it dawned on me that this dear man, like so many others in adult classes, hadn't the slightest idea how to fit the whole Biblical story together chronologically. Saul's name was changed to Paul, that's surely the truth. But the fact that there were two Biblical Sauls, hundreds of years apart on the time line and representing entirely different contexts, had never been clear to my questioner.

As graciously as I possibly could, I explained the difference between the Sauls. And from that moment on, I worked to help that Bible class get a sense of the Biblical centuries and how the story unfolds, B.C. and A.D. When the chronology begins to take shape in a learner's mind, and the books of the Bible are henceforth studied in relation to the flow of time, everything changes. It is a new and creative act for the learner, to construct the history into a sequence with proper spacing between events along the way.

What do these examples have in common? Each one contains a special point at which a student, in interaction with the teacher, the material, or the other students, says or does something that causes active thought to occur.

There is an absence of passivity, of mere absorption by students as if they were blotters. *Moves are made* by teachers and students, and the result is new combinations of ideas—not new for the field of scholarship, to be sure, but new for the students (or teachers) involved.

Human Interaction Related to Ideas

It is not the curriculum materials, or even the general curricular plan that produces these luminous, creative moments I call learning. It is the human interaction in relation to ideas that is crucial. And teachers learn to be open to the myriads of possibilities for such interaction to occur.

In the same year that Whitehead published "The Aims of Education" and other essays that followed it (1929), a giant in the field of Christian education, George Albert Coe, published his book *What Is Christian Education?*[10]

Coe was concerned about the low estate of teaching and learning in the churches, and he wrote about the "creative principle" that must permeate Christian education and revive or produce the realization that education is important even above all other activities of the church.

As a theorist, Coe had a vision of spirituality that would change the character of education in the church—a spirituality that "makes the pupil and the teacher co-agents with the content in determining what is to be."

As he thought about the way in which the church entrusts its teaching ministry to an ill-prepared laity, he sensed that the problem lay in a common view of education as "transmissive"—the passing of a body of saving knowledge from one generation to another in largely verbal form, with the teacher as the principal speaker.

Coe wrote, "We shall not fully understand the almost universal lack of trained teachers until we perceive their task has been to hand on something in which they take no creative or responsible part."

He was right about that. We can still see the great psychic distance that lies between teachers and the materials they use in their teaching. The materials were produced by someone else, through processes of reasoning that the teachers are unable to retrace and possess as their own. The materials only rarely come off the pages, film, tapes, and recordings with that unmistakable ring of authenticity: "This is something that has been lived through by teachers and students, and it will come alive for you in your situation." I believe it is expecting too much of curricular materials to count on them as agents of learning. Only teachers and students together can provide what is missing—the dynamic of active thought, with ideas arranged and rearranged in varieties of combinations unique to every person.

Indeed, Coe was himself overly optimistic about the importance of curriculum. He placed great hope in the work of the Federal Council of Churches, then engaged in curriculum studies that were expected to bring about great improvements and new vitality for Christian education. He could not foresee the Great Depression, followed by the storm clouds of World War II. It was another twenty years before curricular development began to come to fruition, with provision of coordinated studies for church and home.

The churches gave everything they had to the curricular dream from the late '40s through two more decades. No great improvement in teaching competence occurred as a result. Too much trust had been placed in the published materials. Scant attention, by comparison, had been given to the practical subject of *how to teach*. Coe had ideas about it, and he spoke brilliantly of the "project method" that was dear to him. But he himself did not undertake to demonstrate his ideas, saying that this must be accomplished by younger persons.[11]

It has been the same story over and over, in all facets of education. The theorists are strangely willing to leave the practical matters to others. Whitehead wrote: "All practical teachers know that education is a patient process of the mastery of details, minute by minute, hour by hour, day by day. There is no royal road to learning through an airy path of brilliant generalizations."

We would all like to take the "airy path."

More than a decade ago a pastor friend of mine had so wearied of the weekly problems of keeping a church education program going that he mounted his pulpit, announced that the teaching being done in Sunday school was getting nowhere, and declared that he could see nothing on the horizon that offered any hope of improvement.

No doubt it did him good to say what he was feeling, but in the span of twenty minutes he managed to reduce the morale of the entire parish more than he dreamed possible. It was years before that sermon was forgotten. His patience had grown thin, and he looked in vain for the "airy path."

At about that same time, a popular seminary president made a widely quoted speech at a national denominational gathering. It ran something like this: We have cut and pasted enough; we have built enough Palestinian houses; we have played enough games; we have published enough story papers. It's time we got about the business of the church and cut out the nonsense.

It was a popular speech, applauded because he "told it like it is," and the newspapers gave it good headlines. But it did no good at all, because it was not true. The speaker, in search of the "airy path," forgot that teaching requires slow and tedious effort. It really does sometimes involve cutting and pasting (figurative if not actual), and it really does look puny and ineffectual alongside our visions of the Kingdom that is to come.

A wise word of counsel is this: Patience! We must all remember how we learned, slowly and tediously, with much trial and error and with many combinations of ideas. None of us has had a pilgrimage of learning that has been swift and straight as an arrow. We have worked our way through the necessary tedium in our acts of creating. Insight is born of such patient struggle.

Nearly fifteen years ago, I learned of a public school program for evaluating the effectiveness of teachers. It involved a threefold process: study of a definition of teaching by workshop participants so that they could approach the subject from a common frame of reference; actual observation in classrooms by the workshop members, following a period of training in "objective data-gathering"; and finally, a careful rating of teacher performance based on sets of five-level rating scales.

The thing that fascinated me about the process was its attention to the details of what a teacher actually does. It was a fair and open-minded approach to evaluation and offered the possibility of motivating teachers to self-improvement.

Through grants from my own denomination, it was possible to develop a counterpart of the system for use in church education. I coined the name for it: INSTRO-TEACH. This was an ideogram for "Instrument for the Observation of Teaching Activities in the Church."[12]

A corps of leaders was trained and expanded, and the workshops were held throughout the country over a period of several years. The workshop participants would observe classes in both public schools and churches, and they fostered a surprising amount of interchange among church and general educators. I am proud that IN-STROTEACH led thousands of church persons into classrooms for intelligent observation. Boys and girls were observed in their creative tasks of learning, and their teachers were interviewed in depth. An appreciation for the role of teachers was enhanced among church personnel.

But best of all, patience was cultivated. Persons who learned to use INSTROTEACH were aware that teaching and learning are not subject to quick generalizations and ready remedies. The workshops were not especially effective in helping laypersons to know what to do in their classrooms. Other types of follow-up help were needed to accomplish that. But the workshops did open eyes and lead to new insights, and that was enough so far as I was concerned.

Having said these gentle things, having called for patience, I do not want to end this chapter on a wholly irenic note. We need also to be impatient!

As I have hinted, I am impatient with conceptually fuzzy curricular materials that create even greater obstacles for teachers. I am impatient with workbooks and the like that focus on what can only be called inert ideas. I am impatient with administrative structures in the churches that offer so little support to struggling teachers. I am impatient with critics who remain at the theoretical level and who have had no recent taste of what it is like to cope with the tasks of teaching/learning in real classrooms.

Children and young people get impatient too. They long for those luminous moments when something really important takes place—when they are able to create, in the finest sense of that word. Sometimes they despair and become unruly. Consider this observation from George Albert Coe: "A teacher who endeavored to puzzle out an explanation for the irreverence of a group of young people came to the conclusion that they learned it in their Sunday-school."[13] Barred from learning what is ennobling and helpful, our students may learn instead "irreverence." That is a sad outcome, for Whitehead said that religious education inculcates "duty and reverence"!

3 / Developing and Sustaining Openness

For a decade at least, Christian educators have tossed about the words "cognitive" and "affective." The issue, reduced to its simplest dimensions, goes something like this:

Reading and writing, and getting facts and data straightly organized in the mind—even discussions about conceptual frameworks and thinking—are "cognitive." Education, and the church as well, have overemphasized the cognitive, some observers contend. What is needed is more of the "affective."

Nonverbal experiences, sensing and feeling, sharing at an emotional level—all of these, including art and music appreciation—are affective in character. Inasmuch as Christians are concerned with empathy and with such human values as sensitivity to the feelings of others, it stands to reason that this is what we really need.

More often than not, I seem to end up defending the place of cognitive activities in teaching and learning. But I have never denied the importance of the affective; everyone who knows me at all is aware that I cry in movies, weep when saying good-by, and generally lie awake part of every night wrestling with the feelings induced by daily interaction with other human beings.

I suppose what is so frustrating about the cognitive-affective debate is the falseness of the presumed polarity. These two aspects of our existence ("domains" of learning) are no more separable from the total functioning of a human being than are the mind and the heart. No one would think to set the mind against the heart in quite the way some writers and debaters have attempted to set the cognitive area against the affective.

It is a mistake to decide that the cognitive is thinking and that the affective is feeling. The truth is that both our cognitive development and our affective side involve thinking. And they both involve feeling as well.

When we laugh, cry, or dance free in the wind, we are expressing our feelings, to be sure, but we have not left our minds behind. It is part of being human that we literally cannot do that. The creativity of the human spirit depends on our utilizing both thoughts and feelings. The psalms of the Bible are ample evidence for that.

Analytical and Intuitive Thinking

It would be better if we turned this whole issue in a new direction and spoke instead of the differences between *analytical thinking* (such as we do in the careful learning of a mathematical problem, or in the mastery of the syntax of Greek, or in the debate of theological issues) and *intuitive thinking* (such as we do when we listen to music, enjoy poetry, or visit an art gallery). Analytical thinking depends upon structures that can be defended as accurate or inaccurate, provable or not, consistent or inconsistent, applicable or not. No such rigorous standards apply to intuitive thinking, for it is subjective and free to roam about.

If someone were to say to me that Christian education must be concerned with the intuitive as well as the analytical (and vice versa), I would surely agree. A host of good arguments can be mustered for recognizing the vital necessity of both in the church. The apostle Paul's comments concerning "tongues" in the early church, said as much. (See I Cor., ch. 14.) The tongues are ecstatic utterances welling up *(intuitively)* from the joy of the gospel, but they require interpretation *(analysis)*. We seem to have to work all the time at achieving this balance between the intuitive and the analytical.

More than a century ago, the Rev. James McCosh, president of the College of New Jersey (now Princeton University), wrote a landmark book, *The Intuitions of the Mind Inductively Investigated,* an incredibly impressive treatment of the mind-body relationship.[14] He speaks, for instance, of the news that comes regarding the death of a person. For one who does not know the deceased, the information is received as simple data—one more death among the many that are sure to occur. But to a dear friend of the one who died, the news produces an entirely different effect; grief and sympathy are natural responses. The one reaction is more analytical; the other more intuitive. But both are what he calls "mental action." The mind is "that which moves itself," and it moves in a plurality of ways, depending upon the individual's state of being and relationship to others.

One is reminded of McCosh's work these days when the clinical psychologists discuss the right brain/left brain phenomena. Much more work will be done in this area of research, but for the time being we are aware that the left brain appears to be the locus of analytic skills—reading, writing, arithmetic. The right brain is the center of intuitive functioning. The two sides of the brain, through the connective fibers called the *corpus callosum,* are able to collaborate in normal individuals. Both come into play in our daily activities.

The recently popular book *The Dragons of Eden* includes a review of right-hand and left-hand research and speculation. It is important to note where the author, Carl Sagan, comes out.[15] He writes: "The creative act has major right-hemisphere components. But arguments on the validity of the result are largely left-hemisphere functions."

And again: "I think the most significant creative activities of our or any other human culture . . . were made possible only through the collaborative work of the left and right cerebral hemispheres." He is saying that it is essential to have both the analytical and the intuitive for something that is *creative* to occur.

The Atmosphere of Learning

The implications of the analytical/intuitive dimensions for education are tremendous. The main issue is not *which* to regard as important—both are! I believe that the principal problem is a matter of making available to the learner an atmosphere of *openness* that provides opportunities for ready access to what is needed for creating—both analytical and intuitive "raw material," so to speak—and freedom to put these together collaboratively.

For most lay observers, this issue of openness in education relates to quite visceral concepts of "how school should be." It is one of the most volatile aspects of debate about education in many communities, and often it has been dealt with at a purely emotional level. The church has a vital stake in the debate's outcome, in my opinion, and perhaps a really constructive contribution to make.

It is an organizational matter, in a way. (One might even say it is the "politics" of education.) We have to work at openness in these areas: Relationships between teachers and students; teachers' attitudes toward learners' makeup and personal needs; strategies for interaction among teachers, students, and content.

To get at what is meant by openness, we must look at its opposite: the atmosphere in which things are closed. In a school where subject matter is taught for its own sake, it is the simple obligation of the students to conform to the disciplines exacted of them.

In such a setting, all students engage in the same activities at the same time, with teachers directing and their classes moving along in concert according to plan. The best opportunity individuals have to pursue their own interests, or to exhibit their personal talents, is in extracurricular activities or in the preparation of special projects (papers, reports, or independent studies approved by teachers).

Most of us now in our adult years accepted this "closed" aspect of school life as a foregone conclusion. We knew of no alternative. Certainly there was no alternative to it in Sunday school.

But as we all know, in American schools there has traditionally been a degree of humaneness that took some of the sting off the "closed" quality of day-to-day operations. There would be the teachers who gave special attention to individual students after hours. Or times in class when the lesson plan was laid aside for a warm, friendly discussion focusing on students' questions and concerns. Many a self-contained classroom that could have been the scene of drudgery was instead a joyful place of cooperative labor. High moments of communal sharing would come, and these were savored by graduating seniors and recalled at homecoming years hence. Those same qualities would often appear in Sunday classes as well. The fellowship would outweigh the quality of the teaching, and it could be honestly said that it was better to attend than to be absent.

When we speak of "openness," we mean a conscious effort to look upon learners as individual creators (makers, builders) of their educational experiences. Teachers in such a school or classroom are concerned to be *present* to their students, asking: What have they made out of life so far? Where is the evidence of what these persons are now creating?

Some years ago I heard Dr. Martin Marty tell about a course in church history for which he was responsible at the University of Chicago.[16] As I recall, the class included about forty students. At the beginning of the first week, he turned to a student in the front row and asked: "What's your story? Who are you? And where did your people come from?"

In reply, the student told about his ancestry, his family's venture to America, and his own place in the scheme of things.

Dr. Marty decided to ask each student to do the same —to tell the story behind his or her identity. He found, to his considerable delight, that he had in those forty students some kind of link with virtually every culture and religion on the globe. In microcosm, the history of the modern world was gathered in that classroom. It resided in the students themselves. He took the time to be *present* to their identities—to find out, to listen, to record the data. The rest of the semester's classwork was shaped by that initial process of sharing. As Dr. Marty dealt with various aspects of history over a period of centuries, he was able to link the data of subject matter with the personal pilgrimages of his class members.

What an exciting way to teach history. This is a kind of openness in which an observer of higher education can exult—a serious effort to "begin where the students are."

I think back nearly thirty years to my brief pastoral ministry in which I did considerable teaching. If I were to do it all over again, I would pursue the same patterns, only with more intensity and with a better understanding of what I was about.

I went calling on all the people in their homes, not in order to say or to promote something, or to ask them to serve on boards or committees. I went in order to be present to the parishioners. I heard what was going on in their lives, and I saw where the children lived, played, and slept. I found out who the good gardeners were, which persons could sew a fine seam, which persons had the prize recipes to share.

The pastoral calling taught me many things. I discovered a first cousin of Ernest Hemingway, who showed me precious letters from Papa himself! I listened in the barber shop, and in the J. C. Penney store. I stopped at the rail-road station to observe the retired railroaders getting out their watches just as the Burlington Express came through, right on schedule.

From these daily excursions I was able to discern what the people of that parish had *made* of life. They had used what was available to them to create their imperfect world views. We all have limited vision—seeing "through a glass, darkly" (I Cor. 13:12). But any successes I may have had, as a teacher/learner in the community, were surely due to this openness I tried consciously to cultivate.

What I am stressing is that *intuitive* insight comes into play in setting the stage for learning. Learners are enabled to be the creators they are capable of being when teachers and planners are present to them and are careful to culti-vate an openness to where they are.

Many of the things we study in church classes (from Scripture and from other sources) require analytical skills. We have to be able to discriminate between time-tested truths within our heritage and ideas or notions that are alien to these. For instance, in the Jonestown tragedy in Guyana in 1979, hundreds of persons blindly took their own lives in a cultic ritual. We all saw acutely the need for teaching persons to make independent judgment. It is not something that is done without training and practice in logic and debate.

So, when we speak of the need to utilize both the intui-tive and the analytical (both left and right sides of the brain), it seems to me that a lot of the problem is related to how teachers view learners. Are they open to the total personhood of each student?

I think of a tenth-grader who attended one of our labo-ratory classes in Georgia one winter day. When asked for his evaluation of the experience, he said, "I liked it; the teachers took time to get acquainted with us!" That struck me as interesting because it had been only a fifty-minute class, and not more than ten minutes had been used for the "getting acquainted." I pressed him to explain what he meant: "Well, all our teacher at church has said to me lately is, 'Why weren't you here last Sunday?' "

Probably without intending it at all, that teacher had given this student the idea that class attendance was more important than *he* was. It's the difference between a closed view (school for school's sake) and the warmth of human openness.

Just as I was writing this, the newspapers reported on a court case in Bavaria, West Germany. A teacher was convicted of slapping a student in class. But letters to the editor of Munich newspapers were indignant. Citizens believed it was perfectly all right for teachers to exercise corporal punishment—to slap when necessary.

When teachers are open to intuitive perceptions of the learners entrusted to them, most discipline problems disappear. Not all, but most. Many of our discipline complaints are due directly to the closed atmosphere in the sense I have been describing it: class attendance is presented as an end in itself, and the learner must fit the system.

The Open Education Movement

A genuine concern to make educational effort inclusive of the students' total world led to the open education movement following World War II. Teachers who had learned to work productively with their students in bomb shelters and in other innovative settings during the blitzes of London were not content to return to school-as-usual. They sought to develop methods of teaching that would utilize community resources and provide students with wider ranges of choice as they pursued the essentials of the curriculum.

That expression, "open education," caught hold especially in the United States, where it represented a fresh effort to change time-honored patterns of staffing, sched-

uling, and even the architecture of schools. Open classrooms, with miles of carpeting and no walls, or so it
seemed, were part of the movement. The term "open
court" became commonplace, and so did "learning centers," or "learning stations."

Everyone hoped that teachers in open schools would be
better able to relate to each individual ("individualized
instruction" was another watchword of the movement).
The possibility of humanizing the school setting was envi-
sioned so that staff and students would work together in a
common enterprise of teaching/learning.

A few years ago I met the wives of two British army
chaplains. Both were teachers in West Berlin's British sector. To make small talk, I said, "In America these days we
are really attempting to take seriously the 'open education' that began in your country."

One of the women stared with beady eyes. "We don't
think much of it ourselves," she said, turning away from
me.

I have listened to all sides in the open education contro-
versies that have sprung up all around. And I am convinced that here we have another instance of the failure
to think things through before going all out for innovation.
Many good and wonderful things have been accomplished
in open schools; but wherever this has been the happy
outcome, one can always find in the background skilled
planners who are forever testing their intuitions with analytic rigor. They work like dogs to make the open education approach work. It will not work without the hardest,
most consistent, and diligent effort—and planning is at the
root of the matter.

One of the most fascinating phenomena, in the public
school scene, is the flip-flops of commercial publishers during the last two decades. When programmed instruction
packages first came on the market, they were "guaranteed
to teach."

Along came the emphasis on open education, with the

humanistic educators speaking of it as a step toward the renewal of person-centered education. Those very same programmed packages were then advertised by the publishers as "ideal for the open classroom"!

When in the last few years, the new hue and cry was "back to basics" (because supposedly the open classrooms didn't "work"), what do you suppose? Those same programmed packages were now advertised by those same publishers as "perfect for basic education."

This sort of thing is symptomatic of the difficulty involved in designing and executing an open classroom approach. Here are some of the areas that require hard labor:

Teachers must have extensive *planning meetings.* In these meetings, plans have to be laid for all the learning centers that will be made available to students, for all group experiences, and for all times of evaluation with individuals. And other topics that will receive attention will be "team effort" (deciding which teachers will undertake which leadership roles); record-keeping (determining how staff members stay abreast of what students are doing and finishing), and public relations (interpreting the school activities to the community, especially parents).

Teachers must *adapt published materials* to the needs of their students. No canned program is going to work perfectly, and especially if it was designed outside the open education model to start with. No one can begin to guess how many millions of dollars were wasted on gimmicky hardware and other programs during the height of the federal aid to education in the '60s. Poke around in the closets of school buildings, and you'll find the evidence in abundance.

And teachers must work with students on *original projects* related to the students' expressed interests. Such effort can be wonderfully rewarding. But it takes its toll in larger schools. The system breaks down when staff members become lax and are no longer closely involved in the day-to-day planning and designing. Vigilance is the watch-word if an open school is to survive.

I have watched one such school with keenest interest from the day it was built. At first, the open space was somewhat overwhelming. From a central planning area, teachers moved out into quadrants and worked with small groups of students. The principal was called "instructional manager," and he, too, was involved daily in teaching.

Staff turnover was high; as original teachers left, the problems of communicating with parents increased. The school took on a laissez-faire quality. One could find older students lolling about, hardly pursuing anything with real interest.

So the result was predictable. More structure was sup-plied. Cabinets and dividers separated areas of the school, and teachers were functioning rather like their colleagues in self-contained classrooms. The principal was called "principal" once again. An original dream has all but dis-appeared.

Some American experiments with open education have led to near-chaos. These publicized episodes have given the whole movement a bad name in some quarters. Legiti-mate concerns of taxpayers have led to the plea, "Let's get back to basics!"

Nothing is wrong, of course, with staying close to the basics. Students need to learn how to read, how to write, how to think critically, how to do mathematical opera-tions. These basics can be learned—and learned well—in open classrooms. But if the classrooms turn into chaos, making it difficult for students to concentrate, it is possible that the basics, like everything else, will be neglected. That is just what has happened in some cases.

I believe it is important for sensitive Christian educators to know exactly what is happening in public education in their communities and to get involved! We need to help defend what is worth preserving and developing; more often than not, our insight is needed to defend rather than to attack. Schools and good teachers are fragile; we need to make common cause with all who are doing a credible job.

Oddly, the blame for the failure of the open education movement is often laid at the door of John Dewey, who was without a doubt the greatest educational theorist in our history. Dewey would be totally appalled by classroom chaos. He said repeatedly that the purpose of education was to unite *interest* and *effort.*[17] He said that the purpose of education is to produce in students a concentration of effort rather than a dissipation of it. So much of what was going on in the closed atmosphere of classrooms that he knew about was causing dissipation of effort. A student would flit from one subject to another, laboring at one workbook for a while only to have to turn to another assignment, equally tedious and irrelevant to the student's milieu. So Dewey wrote and spoke of the need to help students concentrate—to be thorough, to be truly scholarly.

Chaotic conditions in a classroom or open court school will contribute to dissipation rather than concentration. Dewey cannot be blamed for what goes wrong in such situations, for he didn't prescribe laissez-faire. He prescribed attention to intuitive judgment, on teachers' part —intuitions about how to meet learners where they are.

Open Education in Church

In writing all of this about public education, I haven't forgotten that I am a church educator. Open education has been tried in churches as well—in Sunday schools and in other settings. It has the potential for being more successful in church than anywhere else, I suspect. Here are factors to consider:

1. *Attendance patterns.* Many churches, especially smaller congregations, have low enrollments in certain grade levels. It is possible, in the open classroom arrange-

ment, to combine grades quite effectively. Older students can be helpful to younger ones. Also, every church knows about the students who attend sporadically. The open classroom, with learning centers that deal with only small segments of subject matter, can be used effectively with these casual attenders. They will get something from their participation, but they will not interrupt the sequence and pace for others who attend on a consistent basis. Teachers are not obliged to review continually. And students who arrive late to class can take up where they like, in the learning centers, without disturbing others. Early arrivers can go right to work when they get to class.

2. *Teacher planning.* A team of church teachers can meet for a period of intensive planning and assign tasks to be accomplished; they know that their work is finished for a few weeks. All they have to do is relate to students as the learning centers are used, and be prepared to help students report on their work.

3. *Space.* Church buildings often lend themselves readily to the open classroom approach. Many classrooms are too small to allow for the most effective teaching. When a group of classrooms is used for learning centers, the rooms can be utilized so much more imaginatively.

But now for words of caution. Teachers cannot expect that the open classroom style will be universally effective, week after week. It is best, in my opinion, to utilize the approach for a few weeks, then shift to some large-group activities or other programs. Then, when the next season of learning centers is announced, students will be prepared to return to the approach with enthusiasm once again.

Teachers must avoid planning activities in the open classroom that take on an elaborate "carnival" atmosphere. Some "happenings" staged by teams of teachers were so showy in character that they fizzled after a time simply because no one could keep up that sort of fever-pitch excitement. It is far better to make learning centers simple and appealing; a center that cannot be stowed away in a small box is probably too complicated.

In laboratory settings through the last few years, I have observed some highly effective open classroom sessions, usually combining several grade levels. Often, we have had intergenerational groupings, with grandparents, parents, and young students of all ages (preschoolers through adolescence) enjoying the activities together. Sometimes the teachers who did the planning have thought that certain centers would be most appropriate for children, only to find oldsters delighting in them. And sometimes children engage happily in activities that are quite adult.

The remarkable thing about the learning centers used in an open classroom at church is that one can provide for a wide variety of types of learning activity, while concentrating on a single theme. For instance, the concept of *neighbor* is a Biblical as well as a political, economic, and sociological topic. Students working on this theme can be involved in painting, writing, singing, composing, reading, and discussing—all in the same room, each person working at his or her own pace and in his or her own style. When the time comes for the entire group to share what the members have found out, the interchange among the learners can be exciting indeed.

The process allows for openness in a genuine sense:

Teachers can engage in conversation with small groups of students, or with individuals.

Students can interact freely with one another as they work in the centers.

The element of choice is present so that students may create at their own levels of ability and interest.

Because of the short-term character of religious education programs, the teachers can work to arrange classrooms conveniently and attractively. No one tires of the task if everyone helps with the housekeeping.

Most curricular materials published by the denominations can be adapted to the open classroom, but few have been designed imaginatively for such an approach. The best learning centers call for some kind of creative, interactive work on the part of students who visit them. They need to be designed, written, and set up after having been tested out with a few learners. Teachers learn, by trial and error, how to do this—and how to make adaptations as they go along.

My observation is that most students in church classes that use the open approach, with learning centers, end up concentrating on certain activities that appeal to them. When they have done these thoroughly, they begin to learn. There is little flitting from one center to another.

The obvious benefit of the whole open education effort, utilized in the church, is that it provides a way to combine the analytical and the intuitive. That is true for both teachers and students. Lots of concentrated thinking, writing, and speaking can occur in the classroom. But also, there will be a chance to be quiet and reflective, to relate to persons in nonverbal ways, and to engage in activities that are surely connected to the left-brain hemisphere.

It isn't so much that the content or resources for teaching are radically altered. The open education movement is principally a way of organizing to allow variety and individualization to occur. The method is, in many respects, better suited to the church's educational needs than it is to the unwieldy systems of public schools. Smaller groups, shorter class periods, and teachers who are free to concentrate on planning for their students—these we have in the churches, and hence we can make more effective use of the openness.

To be sure, open classrooms in church will invite the same kinds of "back to basics" criticism from some quarters. The freedom of movement, the variety in activity, and the "fun" aspects of it will strike some observers as suspect. It isn't "like church school should be." But if it can be shown that students are learning, and doing so with greater application and thoroughness, would this not be a reasonable refutation of such criticism? I believe that in time, with more attention to the process, we can show the values of open classrooms.

Openness in the Classroom

But the openness, the variety, and the individualizing of learning can happen in self-contained classrooms as well. I shall never forget a public school teacher in Nashville, Tennessee, who was doing a remarkable job in creating a wide variety of learning activities for her social studies class. They were working on a study of the fifty states, learning about the capitals, the chief products, the regional and climatic differences, and so on. The teacher had personally collected through the years a great assortment of resources about the states—maps, clippings, postcards, slides, and the like. These she had combined with items from the school library.

All around the classroom the students were in teams of two or three, poring over these materials and accomplishing prodigious amounts of work. They made entries in their notebooks, or they visited with the teacher about what they were discovering; she had wisely built in a variety of methods of feedback.

When I talked with the teacher afterward, I said to her: "You were providing such a variety of activities. The students were able to relish their work; it was a delight to watch. And I thank you for demonstrating something that we could surely use in the church as well."

She looked totally surprised. "How?" she asked. "I am a Sunday school teacher, but I wouldn't know how to adapt this approach for use in my church!"

I suggested, on the spur of the moment: "Well, think of those journeys of the apostle Paul that illumine most of the New Testament. Couldn't you pull together lots and lots of material from a variety of sources about those journeys, just as you did about the fifty states? Students in the church class could work with the bits and pieces and enjoy reporting to you in the same way these students in public school did."

The teacher smiled, thanked me, and said: "I never thought of that. And I wouldn't have if you hadn't spoken about it."

Interesting, isn't it? For many persons, teachers included, the whole idea of openness—and deliberately planning for it—has to be reconsidered in every new context. For some persons it is all right in public school but not in church; for others, it may be all right to try something in church school but not in the public sector.

When I attempted to teach in a theological seminary, over a three-year period, I discovered that graduate school is yet another context in which the "closed" approach is often considered the best, even the only method of teaching and learning.

We designed for theological students two courses that were filled with options for individual learners. In one course on church curricula, planned to familiarize the students with the kinds of materials they would likely be using in their parishes, we prepared twelve "modules" of work to be accomplished in the semester. Six of these were to be done in a specific order, but the other six could be done as electives; students were asked to complete at least four of them. Within each module, students had a choice as to how they would go about their work. For example, they might prepare a tape recording or write a paper. (One student decided to write a paper and then record it on tape!)

I had expected that the dean or the faculty would look askance at this course, but they were quite content to ignore it altogether. I was *not* prepared for the students' reactions.

I allowed the class to determine how often we would meet as a total group, and to select the time of meeting. There was a lot of effort, on my part, to be open to the students' preferences and differences in style.

But it didn't go well. We tried several times, and it never "perked." One day I said to a small group of the seminarians: "I don't understand what is wrong here. I have tried to take seriously your complaints about the 'grind' of graduate school. I have accommodated to your needs and have offered you lots of options. This could be a dull lecture course in which I would lay out the details of these church curricula day after day and then give you an exam. I can't believe you would like that. So what's the matter?"

There was silence. And then a member of the senior class replied quietly: "Mr. Bowman, we haven't learned to manage our own learning. You're asking us to make choices, and we aren't accustomed to making choices. It feels uncomfortable."

Well, that was the crux of the matter. Openness had never been an accepted part of their educational careers. I believe that the senior was telling the truth. And I also believe that it is an indictment of education in general. How does one provide for both the analytical and the intuitive if the system is largely structured to make teachers the managers? As God's co-laborers, as creative human beings, students deserve a chance to share in the management of things; and that's the only way I can see creative acts we call learning taking place on a consistent basis. Lots of "education" produces only a minimum of real learning.

It seems to be a fact that learning—either at the time it is occurring or in retrospect—is regarded as a pleasurable experience. It is good and satisfying to be able to say, "I learned . . . ."

One doesn't have to believe in Skinnerian reinforcement theory to say that learning is pleasurable. This is a Christian idea. Some sort of victory, of triumph, is involved when we learn; that is, the human spirit prevails over real or potential adversity, testing, or defeat.

"I have learned," said the apostle Paul, "in whatsoever

state I am, therewith to be content" (Phil. 4:11). He was not making a case for indifference to social ills or injustice. He was simply stating that he could take what came, in his struggle, and make creative use of it—thorn in his side, shipwrecks, lashings, imprisonment. It was all a part of the learning.

Sometimes you hear it said, "I have learned that you cannot trust anyone." Or, "I have learned that society is rotten to the core." Or, "I have learned that there is no more hope." These statements, in the final analysis, are surely cries for attention: Tell me it isn't so! Show me where you can trust and hope. Show me some evidence of human goodness!

The Christian view of learning is victorious. There is a sense of triumph in putting something together for one's self, and for the sake of one's relationship to God and others. The "putting something together" *is* the essence of learning. It is analytical and it is intuitive. Well, yes, it is cognitive and it is affective.

TEACHING / Process of Activating

> And he went about all Galilee,
> teaching in their synagogues.
>
> —Matt. 4:23

4 / Defining the Indefinable: Teaching

For many years now, a line from Matthew's Gospel has informed and guided my own ministry in Christ's church: "And he [Jesus] went about all Galilee, teaching in their synagogues and preaching the gospel of the kingdom and healing every disease and every infirmity among the people" (Matt. 4:23).

Compare this summary statement about Jesus' threefold ministry with Matt. 9:35 and 11:1. In all three instances "teaching" comes first.

If we understand that all Christians are summoned to a vocation of ministry (or service), then that ministry is properly viewed as an extension of the work of Jesus Christ. He is making "all things new," and that creative work of our Lord, in which we are co-laborers, fundamentally involves *teaching*. All Christians are, in some degree, teachers.

In my own understanding of our calling in Christ, it is possible to organize all our undertakings of ministry under the headings of teaching, preaching, and healing. Teaching informs our faith and establishes the character of our Christian community. Preaching keeps alive the dramatic nature of the good news that has invaded our scene in Christ Jesus. Healing is the divine mission of God's people —healing not only the wounds of body and all our sicknesses but also the bitter rifts of human conflict, injustice, and sin-ridden existence. One can easily classify every activity of Christians, or of the church, under one of these headings.

Why are we hesitant to place stronger emphasis on great, pivotal words such as teaching, preaching, and healing? To me, a "Committee on the Ministry of Teaching" is a much stronger, more demanding title for a group concerned about teaching and learning than the fairly innocuous term "Christian Education Committee." A committee with the latter name nearly always ends up trying to define its role and seeking to undertake more than it can accomplish.

We are not always clear in our churches when we use the words "preaching" and "teaching."

Since Vatican II, the Roman Catholic Church has been giving serious attention to both words. The documents of that ecumenical council provide exciting definitions of preaching, and they call for a renewal of the preacher's attention to this vital function as explication of the Word for the modern listener. I believe that the sixteenth-century Protestant Reformers would have been more than pleased with these enlightening statements on preaching.

Just as this book was being written, the long-awaited final text of a catechetical directory, with guidelines for all who teach in the Roman Catholic churches, was being published.[18] It was preceded by a statement from the American bishops, widely studied, under the title "To Teach as Jesus Did." That statement affirms Christians' duty to be faithful teachers.

Proclaiming the Word

Protestants, and especially those in the Reformed tradition, have always placed great emphasis upon the act of preaching. One has only to study the documents of the Reformed churches to see clear evidence of this; the Matthean order of "teaching and preaching" is almost invariably reversed. One finds innumerable references to "preaching and teaching." Things will be what you name them, and the order of the naming seems to represent priorities. Preaching is, for the Protestants, a first duty of the church's ordained leadership. The laity expect it.

One can summarize briefly how preaching became a central focus.

The Reformers were concerned to inform people of the gospel message. They believed that this message had been omitted or obscured for the common people, most of whom were unable to read and write and lived in subjection to the terrors of ignorance. The pulpits of the Reformers became the locus of instruction; pastors, who possessed the Scriptures (the people still did not, for printing was in its infancy), *taught* from pulpits on those occasions when it was possible for the people to assemble for listening. The public utterances from pulpits, which were called "preaching the Word," were clearly efforts to teach. The sermons were long and minute in detail. The administration of sacraments was totally subordinated to the preliminary instruction from the preachers.

In many parts of this country, to this day, the minister is referred to as "the," "my," or "our" *preacher.* It is expected that the sermons from that spiritual leader's lips will be instructive—in the Reformed tradition. In America, at least, the Catholics are influenced by this dominant Protestant view of preaching; they, too, will engage in critiques of their pastor's sermons by asking, "What is he teaching?"

Recently I attended a Sunday morning worship service led by a well-known preacher in my own denomination. It turned out that he was presenting the fifth in a long series of "sermons" based on selected passages from the book of The Acts. The people in the service held pew Bibles and followed the texts as the pastor provided enlightening expositional notes on the Scriptural material. He was not concerned, apparently, about any kind of homiletic structure. He spoke longer than most ministers do, and I caught myself feeling restless. I was a captive, alongside the others, in a teaching-by-lecture situation labeled "sermon" in the printed order of worship. But I was admitting to myself that this is a longtime Reformed tradition. Preaching is the important word, and it appears that the pastor's view of preaching is often simply that this function *is* teaching from the pulpit.

The late C. H. Dodd, New Testament scholar, stressed the distinction in Scripture between teaching (*didachē*, from which comes our word "didactic") and preaching (*kērygma*, which means "proclaiming, announcing"). In recent years, a good many writers have tended to reject Dodd's work, claiming that it makes too discrete a distinction and that the texts do not warrant his conclusions. I will leave that to others, but from a commonsense point of view we must still ask: Why two words? If preaching is simply another instance of teaching, why would there be a conjunction between them—teaching *and* preaching?

Everything I have read in recent years tends to muddle the question. Most writers, if they make a distinction between preaching and teaching, do so by acknowledging only that it is a matter of "emphasis." One can possibly say that preaching is less emphatically a work of teaching because of its obvious limitations (time, lack of interaction with listeners, and the like). And similarly, teaching is less emphatically preaching because it lacks the setting in which sermonizing normally occurs.

But I am not satisfied with the muddling. It seems to me that preaching is primarily a sharing from the heart, a retelling of good news for that day in which the preaching occurs. On the Sunday I heard the "sermon" mentioned above, the minister said not a word about the world I had been living in all week. President Carter was in the Middle East, the Iranian nation was in turmoil, and a host of other concerns were on my mind. I needed to hear some good news. In fact, I need that every day. It seems to me that it should be possible for persons who "preach" to proclaim

anew how they see God at work in the affairs of humankind. That is a mark of preaching—it must be preemi-
nently *contemporaneous.* I did not say extemporaneous. It
must be another forth-telling of the Creator's involvement
in creation—a re-presentation of Immanuel, God with
us.[19]

Parenthetically, it can be pointed out that the position
of the homily in the Roman Catholic Mass is ideally suited
to the foregoing definition of preaching. The Liturgy of
the Word continues as the people ponder the readings
from Scripture. The pastor now preaches, pointing in his
homily to the good news. And the next impulse of pastor
and people is to eat and drink at the Lord's Table, drama-
tizing anew the joy of the living Christ's presence among
us. Preaching is transition from the Word written to the
Word dramatized in the Sacrament.

Equipping to Hear and Respond

In contrast to preaching, which warms the heart, teaching is a patient labor of equipping people to hear and
respond. Teaching is a form of *being with* learners that
can never be fully accomplished from pulpit or lectern. It
is something else altogether to engage in the work of a
teacher.

Jesus is portrayed in the Gospels as primarily a teacher.
In his teaching, he is among the people in a way quite
different from that of the prophets and John the Baptist.
In fact, I believe we can assume that Jesus' own preaching
would not have been altogether different from that of
John—it was an announcement that the Kingdom of God
was at hand, that the awaited time of fulfillment for the
people of God was upon them. This was hearty, comfort-
ing good news.

So it is no surprise that the Gospel writers do not record
again the essential content of Jesus' Kingdom-preaching,
since it was contemporaneous and very much like what

John had said. What they sought to preserve was the outline of his *teaching*, for this was not merely a contemporaneous announcement; it was timeless. It was like no other teaching that had been experienced; it lighted fires to the lives of persons and became a means by which they were to see themselves in a new light. It was Spirit-filled teaching.

What good reason is there for calling Matt., chs. 5 to 7, the "Sermon" on the Mount? The text clearly states that Jesus sat down and began to teach, with authority. Must that Teaching on the Mount be labeled "sermon"?

One can argue convincingly, it seems to me, that in the rhythm of our life as the community of God's people, teaching *precedes* preaching. John's message in preparation for the Kingdom fell upon ears that had been sharpened to hear it, through the patient teaching of generations. The announcement that the Baptist brought was welcomed and produced a response because the groundwork for it had been laid. Now Jesus, in the role of Messiah, teaches, preaches, and heals. But his chief work is the ministry of teaching—of preparing the people to take up their daily burdens in a new "life-style" (as we would say). He does so by saying, "You have heard . . . , but I say to you . . . ."

Later, when Peter preached at Pentecost, he did not proclaim the risen Christ in an unenlightened setting. He cited scriptural texts that had been previously *taught* to the people. They were prepared for Peter's message. They could hear the good news because they understood what he was doing with the long-familiar lines from their scriptures. They could relate it all to the teaching of the Messiah, Jesus.

Through the years I have heard so many clergypersons despair of their work of preaching. "What do the people get from it?" young ministers have asked, and they have turned to other aspects of their work with greater zeal.[20]

Perhaps it has not fully dawned on the preachers of our

time that preaching needs to be preceded by strong programs of teaching. The preacher's words fall on barren ground where the people have not first been taught *how* to hear afresh the good news! How to listen, how to weigh and evaluate, how to interpret the lines of Scripture that appear in the sermon—all these "how to's" are the product of careful preparation, of *teaching*.

Semirecognition of this need for teaching is no doubt what leads many a clergy leader to attempt the "teaching sermon," such as I described earlier in this chapter. But the burden upon the sermon/homily is too great, especially in the time that is available. One cannot prepare the people and also proclaim the good news, all in the same ten, twenty, or thirty minutes allotted for sermonizing.

We do not need to be forever muddled in an admixture of ministries. What is plainly needed is a robust, unapologetic ministry of teaching. It is careful and patient. It prepares people—equips them spiritually and helps them to be the creative individuals God wants them to be.

Alongside that robust ministry of teaching we need also a strong and vital ministry of preaching. It should warm the heart, arouse the passions, stimulate the souls of people —convicting them of sin, assuring them of mercy and forgiveness, and offering them the succor and joyous news necessary to get through another day, another week, another year in this time when God in Christ is making "all things new."

Later, I shall speak about the ministry of healing. It is no less vital, nor is it unrelated to teaching and preaching. The three forms of ministry are truly remarkable gifts from God, and it is a privilege to be partakers in any or all of them.

Curious, isn't it, that our education of the clergy still lays so little practical emphasis upon the ministry of teaching? It is unimaginable that a student preparing for ministry in one of our traditional seminaries would be able to complete his or her work without demonstrating competence in preaching. Required courses in homiletics include "practice" preaching, and guest lecturers in the field of homiletics often outnumber all other adjunct faculty.

But teaching receives nothing like that amount of attention. Students may graduate without demonstrating teaching competence at all. Practice teaching is left to hit or miss in the departments of fieldwork or the like. I really do not know what can be done about it, for I see nothing on the horizon likely to produce serious attention to the distinct but at least equally valid ministries of teaching *and* preaching by the same soon-to-be-ordained, graduating seniors!

Many pastors have chosen to specialize in the ministry of preaching, or in forms of the ministry of healing. Few specialize in teaching. In this area of their work, they draw largely on models from their own educational experience. The body of accumulated knowledge on teaching, and how to go about it, is for the most part neglected by church leaders in favor of other, more appealing aspects of research and continuing education.

Most of the teaching in the churches is still done by lay volunteers. We would be lost without them. The longer I ponder it, the more grateful I am for the work of volunteers, many of whom are such extraordinarily creative and gifted teachers. When the Project for the Advancement of Church Education concluded in Arizona, in 1970, one of the test results that interested me most was the high level of creative imagination exhibited by the subjects in that massive research project. It was higher among church volunteers than among Ph.D. candidates.[21]

The laity, if not the clergy, are still keenly interested in the subject of teaching, wondering how it can be done more effectively in our time. Teaching is a virtually inexhaustible concept. To give one's attention to it, or one's life to it, is to find oneself immersed perpetually in new questions, new discoveries, new dilemmas and quandaries.

What Is Teaching?

Teachers and poets have much in common. Every good poet attempts to explain what poetry is. I recall a fascinating course in college in which we examined definitions of poetry writing from the pens of modern American and British poets. None resembled the others, and none was adequate. Poetry is not definable, yet poets write it, to our everlasting inspiration and enjoyment.

Similarly, every committed teacher would like to be able to say what teaching is . . . but the definition eludes us. It is, like poetry writing, an identifiable human activity, but we are never able to box up a definition that will suffice.

Our English language includes other words frequently used interchangeably with teaching, and it is necessary to reexamine these occasionally to see how they are inter-related.

First, consider *instruction*. It comes from a root word that means to erect a visible or logical thing. When we instruct, we build a structure. (The "struct" is the same in those words.) We establish a foundation of thought and then add, in orderly fashion, the next building blocks of information, data, and theses. As the structure is furnished, the result will stand the test of logical inquiry. The emphasis in instruction is upon *methodical* communication, with a view to transmitting bodies of knowledge and reservoirs of wisdom.

Programmers in the computer industry sometimes speak of instructing the machines. Programs are set up logically, methodically, so that the structure stands up under repeated questioning.

The apostle Paul was surely an instructor. Clues to that are found in his letters, especially in the formidable logic of Romans. Someone once told me that an Oxford don in the field of law would ask each beginning class to unravel the logic of Paul's Letter to the Romans!

Then there is *indoctrination*. It means to imbue with ideas, opinions, and formulas for believing and acting. To indoctrinate is to provide an accepted form of interpretation, approved and passed on for the benefit of the community. Creeds and liturgical material are designed to indoctrinate. There is surely a legitimate place for this; it is not at all a negative concept. Setting firmly in the minds of persons what is of deepest value to a community of believers is a necessary function.

If we say that we do not indoctrinate, we deceive ourselves. Even if we have no creed, no printed liturgies, the unavoidable aspect of indoctrination will still occur in the community. Free churches and evangelical groups who resolutely reject creeds and liturgies will nevertheless exhibit in their common life certain fixed themes, expressed in identical ways in worship and discourse. If one listens to the prayers, especially, one hears certain set phrases that are quite as permanent and formative of the community's self-understanding as any written creed or liturgy.

I grew up in a nonliturgical, rural parish. Each week at Sunday school one of the laypersons would lead a common prayer. I came to know quite well the key phrases that were sure to appear in various persons' prayers. I could, in fact, have offered virtually a verbatim of each one in advance if I had been called upon to do it. It is all still there in my memory after more than forty years. That was indoctrination!

Finally, there is the word *training*. It means, literally, to draw or pull after something or someone. It involves tracking. We seldom stop to think that our railroad "trains" on their tracks were named for a word that had been long in the English language.

The trainer says, "Step in my steps, do as I do, come after me." We could never get through life without training of this kind. From the simple, civil amenities (like please, thank you, hello, and good-by) to the most complex operations of an astronaut, to the correct conduct of a sacramental liturgy—all these things require training.

But *teaching* is greater than any of these three functions. It involves instruction, indoctrination, and training, and is inclusive of all three. Yet teaching is more than all three put together. Teaching implies also openness and choice. The totality of what we mean by teaching puts before us much broader vistas.

Teaching means, in English, to show, to present, to offer for viewing. A teacher takes learners on a journey, directing thought down a variety of paths, conducting, convoying, and guiding in this way and that. Teaching implies two-way communication. The teacher shows and the student reacts to what is shown. How the student reacts will elicit the next appropriate action from the teacher. Teachers may prescribe certain courses of action for learners, but the idea of openness is always there. Coercion is inimical to teaching.

When a teacher is called a "master" or "doctor," these designations are not to be taken lightly—both words imply an ability to survey widely and knowledgeably, and to lead others in diverse ways. It is more than a matter of technics; it is a matter of philosophical acumen born of experience and acquired wisdom. Teachers achieve a certain element of transcendence.

An illustration will serve to pull together what I have been saying.

We are all acquainted with those unheralded heroes and heroines of this land who are called "music teachers." I am speaking of those wonderful persons who have in their homes a piano or two, and who welcome boys and girls individually for weekly or semiweekly "lessons." People still speak of "taking" from such teachers; in every community they are charged with enormous responsibility as stewards of the art of music.

First, there is *instruction*. "Here's how you sit on the bench . . . Here's how the piano is put together . . . Here's how you begin to practice the scales . . . Here's how you use the left and right hands to play." A structure is built for thinking about playing this instrument; in building-blocks fashion, a pupil is furnished with the essentials for digging into the beginner's book (Will it be John Thompson's *Modern Course for the Piano, First Grade Book?*).

Then comes *indoctrination*. "You must not give a full beat to a half note . . . You cannot shift keys arbitrarily in the midst of a piece . . ." It takes a genius to defy the established doctrines of the music teacher. When Debussy began to play differently, his master said, "By what rules are you doing this?" He replied, "By my own rules, to suit my own pleasure." But that was a genius at work, and he could defy tradition only when he first had been indoctrinated with it.

And surely there is *training*. "Here, watch my hands and let me show you how to attack that chord . . . Let me show you what you are doing when you place your foot on the pedal . . . Play it as I am doing. Now let me hear you." Training, training—where would a music studio be without it?

But these aspects of a musical education are not enough. The teacher of music must have symphonies in his or her head. Teachers of music must be attuned to the songs of the spheres, sensitive to the muse (that's where the word "music" comes from!). In short, a music teacher is always *open*—to music. He or she never loses sight of the dream, the love, the ecstasy of this art. Every young hand is potentially the hand of a gifted player, if not a Mozart, possibly a concert pianist. If one teaches music, this must always be in the foreground of one's thinking. Teachers are not empty vessels, they are the dreamers, the seers—seers of what is (realists) but also of what could be (idealists).

A teacher never knows what he or she may be causing to *begin*.

And sometimes teachers are insensitive to what they may be killing or snuffing out. One must be careful to note that overinstructing, overindoctrinating, overtraining—without the "plus" element that combines these and allows for much more besides—can very well quench the spirit of a learner and remove that openness and wonder about which I am speaking. (One is reminded of a popular little book of some years ago: *The Geranium on the Window Sill Just Died but Teacher You Went Right On.*)

Teachers within the Christian tradition should be always opening things up, pointing toward new doors. Our Scriptures and our traditions make that an infinite possibility, for there is always "new light" breaking forth.

I like the imagery of a teacher as a midwife or an obstetrician.[22]

Anyone who has witnessed a birth knows about the role played by these professionals. The attendant at birth is not responsible for all that is involved in the mystery of a new life's entry into the world. But by being present, by helping the first cries to be healthy ones, by assuring that breathing occurs unobstructed, the attendant plays a vital role—spelling often the difference, literally, between life and death. It is as close as one can get to the origin of life. By being present and actively helping, the midwife or obstetrician is involved in a precious beginning.

Teachers as Activators

If we think of learning as an act of creating, then our view of teaching has to fit well with that idea. Teachers are *activators*. They are present to help something to begin, to sprout, to take its first breath. Like midwives, they are not fully responsible for the process, but they are as close to it as they can get. By being present, they can play a role in activating.

I don't know whether I arrived at the word "activating" independently of Jerome Bruner, or in unconscious reflection upon something I read from his book *Toward a Theory of Instruction.* He wrote that "exploration of alternatives requires something to get it started, something to keep it going, and something to keep it from being random."[23] Insofar as teachers are persons who help students to explore alternatives, they are involved in what Bruner calls *activation, maintenance, and direction.*

To play a part in causing something important to begin, in the full recognition that one is not wholly responsible for what went before and for what will come—that is what is meant by activating. Within the limits of language, that seems to come close to describing the essential work of teaching.

When I used the word "activating" in a group of volunteer teachers in an Eastern state, one of them wrote me a note that said: "Your word leaves me cold. Are we teachers nothing but activated charcoal?"

The logic of the note was absurd, but it troubled me nonetheless. "Activated" was a part of that teacher's vocabulary only in the limited sense of a phrase in the marketplace. So there wasn't anything I could do to help the note writer to see how differently I was using the word. Of course, teachers aren't charcoal, being acted upon! They are actors, taking initiative as side-by-side co-laborers with the learners. By virtue of wider experience and stored wisdom, teachers are able to guide and convoy learners, to show alternatives, and to draw upon their subsidiary abilities as instructors, indoctrinators, and trainers. Does that not make sense and place teachers in the same creative role as learners? A theory of teaching, like a theory of learning, rests ultimately on the word "creation" as we understand it in our Jewish and Christian traditions.

To return to Dr. Bruner's view of the teaching act, he believes that a teacher's role is to help students explore alternatives. He adds: "The major condition for activating exploration of alternatives . . . is the presence of some optimal level of uncertainty. Curiosity, it has been persuasively argued, is a response to uncertainty and ambiguity."

The raising of questions, posing of dilemmas, presentation of unsolved problems—these are the tools of a teacher's craft. Students see alternative possibilities: varieties of answers to questions; several ways of solving a posed problem or dilemma. Just below the threshold of frustration, the students experience the right amount of uncertainty. Their curiosity is aroused, and they are off and moving! Something has been started, activated. That is how learning begins. Initiating the process is the teacher's privilege. As Bruner puts it, "knowing is a process and not a product."

Would it be amiss to put Jesus' own teaching to the test of these criteria? His parabolic approach stands up impeccably when weighed by Bruner's thought. Jesus would tell a parable. The hearers would wonder among themselves what it meant. Jesus would answer their questioning with questions of his own, for example, "Which of the three, do you think, was neighbor to the one who fell among thieves?" (See Luke 10:36.)

The parables do offer alternatives that we can continue to explore. They raise just the right amount of uncertainty so that our curiosity is stimulated. We puzzle over them in such a way that we learn. We are led to the creation of a lasting image of the Kingdom of God.

The great questions that lead to learning have no hammered-in right answers. They pose alternatives so that a learner has to make a choice. This element of choice is just as essential in the building of a viewpoint or of a quality of human character and spirit as it is in selecting the right materials for building a house.

The important thing is to furnish minds with what they need to work with in order to deal with alternatives.

Dr. Hulda Niebuhr, of the famous Niebuhr family, is often remembered best for her saying: "Teaching is not just telling people things." She meant by that: Teachers are not dictators, fixing in concrete the answers they expect from their students. Rather, they leave the parable for the student to puzzle over; they pose the question,

"What do you think?" or they provide clear-cut evidence for divergent thinking. Students, with their interest aroused, are then obliged to make a choice.

To put it another way, teachers do not *impose* their views upon their students. They help students to *compose* their own views.[24]

To be sure, teachers do not abdicate their responsibility when students cry: "Help! We don't understand." Teachers impart the necessary information or the essential ingredients for helping students to succeed in solving their problems and coming to necessary conclusions.

How do we go about becoming activators—teachers who set learners' feet on a pilgrimage?

Surely one key to it is to put ourselves back into the shoes of the learners. We must explore each of our own remembered experiences again and again, asking: How did it happen? What did I have to work with? What was I able to make out of the experience? How did I do it?

Working from this reexploration, we then set up the conditions under which such experiences can be replicated for our learners. That is why classrooms are so handy. They bring us close enough together as teachers and students that we can work comfortably at these replicated experiences. The old-time rabbis laid out the scrolls on tables and moved about as the men and boys read from them. As chief learners, the rabbis would point out things to the less-experienced readers. There was an openness to this, a desire to replicate pleasurable experiences of discovery, and a gentle nudge to get something started—to activate the readers!

Sometimes we hear people say, "The Bible teaches . . . ." Well, in a superficial sense that is true. But more precisely, the Bible does not teach by itself; it provides the essentials for us to work with, but the teaching and learning happen in relation to the text only after guided study and historical inquiry! What a lot of nonsense would no longer be imposed on innocent people if we would only propagate this important fact—that the Bible is not in and of itself a teacher absolute. The Scriptures were meant to be pondered "in community" by the people of God to whom they belong. The Scriptures speak authentically when they are mediated through a human ministry of teaching that takes into account adequate background knowledge and skills of interpretation. A teacher needs to be there as the activator, the midwife, to make Bible study a real teaching/learning experience. That is one of the reasons why our work as Christ's ministers is so terribly important.

Teaching quite properly includes sharing personal excitement and enthusiasm with others. That seems to be a hard concept to convey to would-be teachers.

Earlier I referred to my work with seminarians over a three-year period. We had a laboratory type of setting in which we brought the students together with young persons of various age groups. The seminarians were to work in teams in order to design and teach for a period of fifty minutes a group of young people from an age level of their choice. I would always listen with interest as the young theologians would come to the question, "What shall we teach?"

Invariably, I would respond: "Well, how about selecting something you yourselves have learned lately here at the seminary—something about which you are really excited? Choose a Biblical concept, a theological premise, an ethical insight, or an episode from church history. Let it be something that is real to you, vital at this very moment. Then devise a way to teach it to the boys and girls so that they, too, will sense what an important concept or idea this can be."

I was never successful in helping the students to undertake that sort of approach. Always they would abandon the idea after entertaining it briefly. They could not see how something learned in seminary could be taught to children and youth. In the end, they would turn to the "safe" material from the pages of printed curriculum on our resource shelf.

I am still puzzling over why that should have been the seminarians' reaction. It is disturbing to contemplate how minimal the transfer of learning apparently is. Seminary learning is reserved for a mental compartment. The concerns and interests of young persons are in another compartment, so far as I could assess the situation. And never the twain shall meet.

Professional educators and ministers often speak possessively of "our people." They insist that "our people are not yet ready for the kinds of thinking being done by theologians and denominational leaders." Well, if we think of "our people" as forever *not quite ready,* then we deprive both them and ourselves of some of the most exciting possibilities for teaching/learning.

I have a vision of a new type of parish minister. He or she is never guilty of saying: "I don't teach. *My* lay people do that, and they have my support."

This new type of minister says instead: "I am engaged in teaching in this parish. It is a time-consuming, awesome task, but I do it because of the trust placed in me by Jesus Christ, the Master. It's my privilege to work at the task of teaching alongside the gifted people who reside here and who willingly give of themselves to make this mutual ministry possible."

This new type of minister says: "There's a way for me to speak the meaningful word as I teach. I will know more of what the way is when I do more listening. There's a way for me to keep things opening up for the students, and I will not close down and impose my own will. There's a way for me to get beyond the printed page of curricular materials to center in on what the students' own life issues are. There's a way for me to make the education I received in seminary (so exciting and life-changing for me personally) an essential part of what I share with the persons in this parish. There's a way to bring uncompromising scholarship to bear upon the common life of persons in today's world."

My vision is of ministers and laity working together at that indefinable calling known as teaching. The next two chapters will relate to specific details of how this is done.

5 / Stretching Vision for a Lifetime

Studies of human growth and development have made us keenly aware of the differences among persons at the various age levels. Conclusions about young children based upon observation and laboratory types of experiments are especially enlightening. Nothing has affected my own work more profoundly in recent years than the insights gleaned from serious study of Jean Piaget. It is devoutly to be hoped that his investigations will be read and understood for many years to come.

Brain research in the last decade or so has shown that there may be sound physiological reasons for some of the things Piaget found out about infants and children. A three-year-old simply does not have the same brain structure as a ten-year-old. Growth is observable in technical experiments designed to show brain function in relation to perception and problem-solving.

It is not my purpose to deal with age group differences in a detailed way. That has been done adequately by many others who are knowledgeable in this field. It is more important, for now, to raise a flag of caution with respect to these studies.

Without exception, the students of psychology and human development who have laid out their views of the growth patterns we go through in a lifetime have intended to *describe* what they have observed. They collected data, analyzed it, and presented their tentative conclusions.

Years ago, when I first became seriously involved in education, everyone studied the work of Robert J. Havighurst, with a view to finding out what students were like at the various stages of development. Then we all read excitedly the descriptions from Ilg and Ames. Many other names could be added. The work of all of them was intended to be descriptive.

But teachers, both professionals and lay volunteers, tend to look upon it as *prescriptive*. We crave certainty about how to work with the various age levels, and we study the developmental charts for clues to that "right approach" to our classroom work. Because the charts describe how a child or youth of a certain age *tends* to function, it is only a small step to concluding that this is the way they function always. Too readily we decide what ought to be, or what shouldn't be, allowed in the education of persons.

For instance, a detailed growth chart would make clear that six-year-olds do not speak metaphorically and show little evidence of grasping truly poetic speech. From this observable, descriptive knowledge of six-year-olds, many teachers and writers have concluded that first-graders should not hear Psalm 23, with its imagery of God as a shepherd. Moving from the descriptive to the prescriptive, the teachers make a tactical decision—they *prescribe*, "No exposure to Psalm 23 yet; it doesn't fit the age level."

What a pity! Statements about learners in general often become obstacles to the cultural development of deserving children when teachers turn descriptive material about learners into prescriptions for their classroom operation. No one is ever too young to be *exposed* to something as beautiful and universal as Psalm 23!

We should be very slow to decide what children can or cannot do, as individuals. God has created each of them differently, and to say that is not to deny general age group characteristics at all. It's just that any keen observer in a classroom will note that two-year-olds do not all behave in the same way, and neither do thirty- or fifty-year-olds. One of the great contributions of Robert Coles has been his ability to help us see the individuality of persons. He knows from interviews with persons across economic, social, and racial and ethnic lines, that they break out of the role images we are all too prone to assign to them.

Persons of great intelligence sometimes struggle to describe why their public school experiences were stultifying and something of an obstacle rather than an aid to achievement. Often someone will say: "If only the teachers hadn't decided what I couldn't do! I had to take initiative *outside* of school in order to get the books I wanted, to explore the ideas that fascinated me, because teachers thought I shouldn't be doing these things or reading these ideas at *my* age."

Piaget has given little practical guidance about how to direct day-to-day educational experiences for the young, but one can surely read between the lines that he is all *for* broad exposure of children and youth to all facets of life. Just because children and youth will *create* different meanings for themselves as they encounter the "stuff" of culture, is no reason to deprive them of exposure to a wide variety of materials. The meanings will be created differently at later times, and the ledgers get balanced as persons move along in their development.

When I was ten years old I read *Gone with the Wind*. It was wonderful that no one stopped me; I loved the challenge of completing such a thick volume that the whole world (or so it seemed) was talking about in the 1930's. I certainly did not interpret it in the same way I would have had I been an adolescent or an adult, but I learned a lot from reading it. It would have been a most miserable experience for me if my teachers or parents had denied me access to that book. They surely would have had they pinpointed my age level on a development chart and arrived at the prescription: "No adult books yet!"

Age-Level Characteristics

This whole topic has a lot to do with church education, from two sides of the matter:

1. Many church teachers ignore the age-level characteristics. They try to *impose* material on children and youth when they are simply not ready or when they just plain cannot understand.

2. Many church teachers swing too far in the other direction. They take the charts and descriptions so seriously that they *bar* children and youth from exposure to the content of our heritage.

Let us reflect a little further on both of these extremes. The so-called children's sermons is a good place to begin.

In my travels I have heard many children's sermons. I have not the slightest doubt that the ministers and priests who deliver them are persons of goodwill and with well-meant intentions. But they persist in using object lessons that impose adult type of analogies on children. The adults who listen to these will often say, "I get a lot out of the children's sermon," and that's just the point. The minister talks in rather vivid, concrete imagery quite intelligible to adult listeners. But the children are used as a "foil" for this procedure. The children are little more than "objects" themselves. They are expected to know why a bag of garbage, for instance, is like the clutter of human sin; why a cake of ice is like "coldness of heart"; or why a thousand other concrete objects can be cited as analogous in character to the abstract words of religious language.

I must be careful not to be misunderstood. If children themselves are capable of making these analogies, and desire to do so, that's one thing. But when they are a captive audience asked to ponder such material in a service of worship, with an adult gallery looking on, this is something else again. What makes it most questionable is the fact that the practice is called "For Children."

I am willing to wager that children who worship in churches alongside their parents and hear the sermons/homilies intended for a general audience get just as much meaningful content as they would if they were required to gather for a "children's" period with the pastor. In the general liturgy, for the whole people of God, children are free to take what is offered and create from it what makes sense to them. That is their God-given right and privilege. But in the sermons for children, they can exercise their freedom only as an act of resistance to this effort to impose something designed "for them."

Children are not objects. They are not meant to be "objectified" and "used" by adults. Children are entitled to the same subjective freedoms all other human beings deserve—freedom to think things through, to make choices, and to construct meaning in their own ways.

What happens in these imposed sermons is not unlike what happens in classrooms where teachers do the telling, and children do the listening. Teachers impose the conceptual frameworks, and it is the students' lot to accept or resist. Sometimes the resistance has to occur under conditions of guilt; it doesn't feel good to be rejecting inwardly what is said by teachers with considerable emphasis.

George Whitefield, the eighteenth-century evangelist, wrote of his attempts to convert a four-year-old soul on board a ship during one of his crossings to preach in America.[25] We read that with a certain sense of shock; he could not possibly have understood the makeup of young children and attempted such a radical imposition. But similar episodes, possibly more subtle, still occur in religious education. Teachers and clergy insist on forcing issues, imposing cardinal concepts of the faith without stopping to think: How do children think? What are they really like at the different age levels? I am insistent that we have not done nearly enough to emphasize the growth patterns and capabilities of children and youth, especially in the education of the clergy.

And now to return to the other side of the question, especially as it applies to Christian educators and the teachers who have been very serious about the nature of childhood and youth. I will put myself in this group and say we have also erred in yielding to stereotypes of our students rather than looking upon each one as a remarkably unique child of God, created with special combinations of ability and insight.

I have met more than seven thousand boys and girls of all age levels in the last decade. If nothing else, this privilege convinced me utterly that we must not work so hard at devising ways to speak "children's language." Children like us best when we are quite open in their presence and strive to interact with them as co-learners. We should be ourselves (adults), and allow each child or young person to be the same. This eliminates "talking down" or adopting special lingoes, or working hard to be "with it" in our manners of speaking. Infants, children, youth, and adults appreciate most the persons who strive least to cultivate them superficially. Have you noticed how some teachers of preschoolers will adopt a special tone of voice and a sort of false gaiety of manner, because they presumably think this is what young children need from them? To be sure, children need teachers who are deeply interested in their welfare, their ideas, their contributions to a group. But this interest does not have to manifest itself in something artificially cultivated such as a "preschool voice." Children like adults to speak in adult voices, with sincerity and consideration. Vocabularies must be adjusted, of course, but not *too* much. What an embarrassment to hear four-year-olds tossing around words, with joy, that their teachers have avoided as simply "inappropriate to the age level"!

The situation is something of a paradox. We need the descriptions of how people grow and develop and what sorts of things they are "ready" for at the various age levels; at the same time, we must avoid being so orthodox about these descriptions that we end up with a sterile approach to teaching. Students of all ages deserve the chance to grow and develop "off the charts" in marvelous ways of their own devising. Just as libraries should not exist to prevent people from reading, so the developmental charts should not exist to prevent people from exercising freedom to grow as they will.

Free to Investigate

The key to the matter is the freedom to investigate. Learners as creators are entitled to that freedom, wherever it leads them. In church education, it may lead children to explore portions of Scripture that seem "too adult," or it may lead adults to revel in children's books. It may lead adolescents to attend theological seminars with a passion to learn akin to their zeal for musical or artistic or scientific competence. People *can* be described in general ways, and that is good, for "people" is a general term. But individual persons, as Christians surely know and affirm, won't stay in boxes. They burst out and do things in individual patterns that are marvelous to observe and applaud!

To come at it another way, we educators do such a good job of convincing ourselves and others that people are *different* at various stages in their development that we forget to examine certain common denominators among the stages, the things that are the *same* throughout life. One area of sameness is simply that each of us desperately needs to be respected for his or her own worth and individuality. No one seriously wants to be looked upon as only a representative of one's age group. That holds for nursery school students through the so-called "senior citizen" groups (a terrible appellation for human beings, if you ask me).

We like to interact with other persons from the point of view of our own identity, as individuals. When a teacher takes an activating role with students, it has to be on the basis of an ability to see each one as creating in his or her own way.

Whatever else teachers do, they engage their students in *conversation.* The quality of this conversation will stem from their inner views of the students as persons. Even the most formal lecture is conversation of a sort. Lecturers expect their hearers to plot mental interaction of a verbal kind as they listen. I know that this happens; on occasion, when I am lecturing, I will notice someone's lips moving. He or she is composing mental reactions to what I am saying, and the lips are a cue that this process is occurring.

We err if we take conversation for granted. It is something we can learn to do skillfully, and teachers especially should cultivate the art.

Conversation is always *about* something. Ideas, events, people, places, and objects become the grist for our conversation. We speak sometimes of "conversation pieces," items that stimulate curiosity and prompt people to talk with one another. In a way, it is the task of teachers to search for conversation pieces that will aid in the activating process.

In a long-ago Sunday school class, the teacher would display each week a new wall picture, hanging like a large calendar page. Thirteen of these pages were bound together, and they were flipped over, one at a time, to supply a new scene for each week of the "quarter." This picture prompted the teacher's questions and storytelling for each week; it was a conversation piece. At the end of the session, each student received a miniature card (also lithographed in lovely colors) to take home; it was an exact reproduction of the larger class picture, and it also contained printed Scripture texts to be studied or memorized. We smile now at this uniform technique of teaching, but it had its value; the picture was focal, and it caused conversation to begin. Oddly, the students never "peeked" to see what the pictures would be for weeks ahead; that would have diminished the charm of the whole procedure. Everyone preferred to wait for each week's turning of the wall chart.

When public school teachers and preschool staff members bring animals, plants, stones, shells, leaves, and a variety of other nature objects into the classroom, it is for the purpose of causing conversation to begin.

Recently I visited a large church in an Eastern city. It had a huge, multistory educational wing, and I went on an unaccompanied tour to see what the rooms were like. To my great surprise, I found dark, barren scenes—tables and chairs, Bibles lying askew in some rooms, and hardly anything else. When students would file into that building for Sunday classes, I wondered how the teachers would get something important going. Where would conversation pieces be? I am able, fortunately, to contrast that scene with other visits to educational wings where the rooms were a delight to behold: colorful and meaningful bulletin boards, reverently produced exhibits related to the study topics, and materials related to the students' own current progress in classes. The conversation was of high order!

Conversation ideally begins to develop as a human skill in early childhood. Mealtime is a fine setting for cultivating the habit of conversing. Parents talk with each other about the events and issues of the day; children listen and also participate, and they share the happenings of their own lives as well.

Not surprisingly, in many homes today, where television viewing and other activities crowd out the ritual of the family meal, conversation suffers—and both communication and learning are thereby diminished. A correlation exists between children's abilities to converse and their reading abilities. Show me a boy or girl who can carry on an extended and intelligent conversation, and it is highly likely that he or she will be eager to check out books from the library. Reading is a form of conversation, as readers get caught up in the pages and respond inwardly to the enticing ideas supplied by writers.

All these fairly obvious things I am setting down in order to underscore the teacher's activating role. Getting something going by way of conversation is utterly essential to the following aspects of teaching/learning.

Comparing/Contrasting

We learn to distinguish the things that differ by engaging in deliberate acts of comparison. It is fundamental to reasoning and to any creative effort.

When our son was very young, we lived in a large apartment house in Philadelphia. It was about half a mile around the grounds of that complex, and good solid concrete walks had been built all the way. Parked with their noses toward the walks were hundreds of cars that belonged to the people in the apartments. By the time he was three, I would take our boy on a daily walk. We'd talk about all sorts of things, but we would also examine each car. Before long he linked the chevron symbol with the Chevrolets, the special markings of a Buick with that car, and he did the same with Fords, Cadillacs, Volkswagens, and the others. He became an expert at identifying vehicles. It was the beginning of a skill that we use and never abandon for as long as we live—we compare and contrast things and ideas.

Jesus did this in his teaching. His hearers had to make comparisons, ponder the contrasts, and create for themselves a radically new ethic.

We cannot assume that students know the difference between good and evil, between honesty and dishonesty, between genuine and adulterous relationships, between humility and arrogance, until we have provided over and over again opportunities to see the contrasts. Not in generalizations alone or in mere catechetical answers but in concrete examples, vividly presented in a conversation that involves real give-and-take, does real learning take place. Comparing and contrasting are the first stepping-stones to sound reasoning.

Analogy

From the actions of comparing and contrasting comes the skill of *analogy*. An analogy compares one set of circumstances with another having similar properties or qualities. A listener who hears one is able quickly to make the connection and to see how the central concept or issue is clarified in the comparison.

Very young children can make simple analogies. A teacher said to a group of preschool children: "I have magic ears . . . I can hear a tooth growing." And after a pause they began to add their own, analogous examples: "I have magic ears . . . I can hear a smoke go by . . . I can hear a cat's whisker move . . . I can hear the Empire State Building swaying."[26]

The focal idea is that of being able to hear something that is inaudible. Each example is analogous to the others in this respect. It is the simplest form of analogy-making.

As students grow older, they give evidence of being able to do this at a much more sophisticated level. One time I had given a lecture to a group of UCYM students who were meeting at Kenyon College; my address was on the relationship of Old and New Testaments. Our son, by then ten years of age, asked if he could come along. I wondered about the wisdom of his decision, but he sat and listened intently. Afterward, we were going hand in hand across campus to the dining room. Suddenly I heard him saying: "Dad, I was thinking about the Old and New Testaments as you were talking. It's something like the books *Tom Sawyer* and *The Adventures of Huckleberry Finn.* Each one of those books helps you understand the other one." I rejoiced at his insight, of course. From his voicing of this analogy I could tell that something had happened for him: something was activated.

In a laboratory class for junior highs, the teachers supplied students with some "chocolate cheese" and asked them to taste it and comment. One of the boys in the group said: "It tastes sharp and smooth. How odd! How can something be sharp and smooth at the same time?" He was expressing a minor paradox.

A few moments later, the students were asked to look at a group of pictures of the head of Christ and to choose the ones that interested each of them. The same boy selected a painting of Christ that no one else chose as a favorite. When asked to explain, he said: "I like this one because he looks far away and close to us. Now, how can that be? How can he be far away and close at the same time? But that's the way it seems to me." This time, he was expressing a major paradox.

The paradoxical observations in relation to the chocolate cheese and in relation to the painting of Christ were so close together in this student's experience within a class period that you would have to say that this was an example, again, of analogous relationships.

This analogy-making process cannot be *forced*, as is so often the case in children's sermons to which I referred earlier. But when students have begun to show ability in comparing/contrasting, a teacher can begin to offer experiences that will elicit analogies naturally. It is exciting to watch it happen.

Similes

The process is best initiated by using the word "like" so that students can form similes. Similes usually come prior to metaphors in our process of learning.

A church school lesson was repeated experimentally with a number of groups of students in grades 5–6 over a period of a year or so. It was based on I Peter 2:1–10. In this passage, Jesus Christ is compared to the following: *milk* that is fed to newborn babes; the *cornerstone* in a building; the *light* that illumines our way in darkness.

My teaching strategy began as I showed the children a glass of milk, a stone, and a lighted candle. We talked about each of these. What are they used for? What can be said about each one? What would we do with them?

As in all such experiments, the students were wondering what the point could be. They offered their ideas somewhat tentatively and hesitantly. When it was clear that I had exhausted the possibilities for conversation, I projected an overhead transparency containing the passage from I Peter, and I read it aloud as the students followed.

"What do you notice about these lines?" I asked.

In a flash, the students were shouting out: "There's the milk!" "There's the stone!" "And the light he's speaking about must be the candle!"

Then I probed: "How is Jesus like all these things?"

Each student was provided with a write-on slide and a variety of pens and pencils. The group were invited to make individual slides illustrating the meaning of the Bible passage, as they understood it.

In one class, a student who had been quiet during the conversation and the reading added his slide to the collection. It was a circle of beautifully drawn stones, one to represent each class member and the teacher as well—plus another, shaded stone. The student explained: "See, we are all brought together into a circle, and this special stone in our circle is Jesus Christ. That's what I got from the Bible when we read it."

In his own way, he was drawing the analogy perfectly; he could express it best through the medium of slide-making.

A number of the students exhibited frustration with this assignment; they were not yet ready to attempt such advanced analogies. So we learn from such experiences not to force the process; we wait and try again later. Trying to

make the students "see" by telling what *we* observe will
often do no more than complicate the issue; it is like trying
to make a flower bloom before the petals have emerged
fully from the bud.

Even for some adults it is not a simple process to think
analogically.

In recent years I discovered that one of the ancient
practices in the synagogues of Judea was to assign questions like these for general discussion:

How is Torah (the law of God) like oil? How is Torah like
wine? How is Torah like water? like light?

The members of the synagogues could spend hours discussing the relationship between the law's beneficial
effects and the desirable qualities of these common, everyday items enjoyed in a household.

It seemed to me that it would be interesting to ask a
group of the clergy to engage in just such an exercise. I
divided them into small teams and asked them to discuss
these questions quite seriously for at least ten minutes.
Most of the teams found it extremely difficult. They wan-
dered off into descriptions of items in modern terms, saying things like, "Oil is a lubricant for motors"; or, "Light
travels more rapidly than sound"; or, "Water contains a
variety of minerals." None of these kinds of comments
would have appeared in a Judean synagogue conversation
of two thousand years ago. The participants would have
had lusty things to say about the refreshing qualities of
cold water on a hot day in the desert; about the comfort
from a quaff of good wine; about the ability of light to
dispel darkness. It is these latter qualities, together with
many other things we could say about the concrete items
of daily living, which are useful in helping us to describe
the wonderful gift of God's Law—a benefit we did not
deserve but one nevertheless richly bestowed on us for
our good.

Why do people find it hard to work with poetic expressions (and that is what so many good analogies are!)? Be-

cause we are all so impatient to get on with abstract discourse, I suspect. But the Biblical heritage that informs all that we are and do in the church asks us, repeatedly, to confront the simple but profound questions such as: How is the law of God like milk? And how, indeed, is Jesus himself like milk for newborn babes? This sort of imagery is at the very heart of our teaching enterprise. It is what we have to activate in the learners.

Metaphors

From stories, similes, and parables, it is a necessary final move to consider the metaphor in our teaching/learning. A metaphor involves analogical thinking, too, but in a shorthand sort of way. The "is like" has disappeared so that A *is* B. From Psalm 23 we derive the metaphor, God is a shepherd. We do not take that literally at all. We mean that as a shepherd cares for and tends and guides sheep, God cares for and tends and guides people. So we speak also of Christ the Good Shepherd. And think of all the metaphors for the nature and work of Jesus Christ! He is the Rock of Ages; he is the lily of the valley; he is the bright and morning star; he is the door. Again, none of these is meant to be taken literally. We are able to make the leaps of interpretation that supply all the qualities of each physical object in the list of examples, then quickly apply those qualities to Jesus Christ, affirming that indeed he *is* those very things! It is a poetic way of thinking and speaking that is very near to the heart of faith itself. To be able to revel in the metaphors is to be able to sense what is of greatest spiritual depth.

Young children seldom do metaphors. One time I read aloud to a group of first-graders the line, "I am the light of the world." I said to the children: "That is what Jesus called himself. What do you suppose he meant?" There was a silence, and then a delightfully honest child looked at me with eyes fixed, and he said, "Mr. Bowman, that's too hard for first-graders." The tension was relieved, and we moved on to something appropriate.

But then, many adults seldom do metaphors either.

What seems to be involved is a two-level process of thinking. At Level 1, we are able to make descriptive statements about objects and ideas. To form a metaphor requires that we think at Level 2, engaging in a shorthand form of expression in which the meanings are implicit.[27] A metaphor, as I have pointed out, catches up all the qualities of something concrete and deftly ascribes these same qualities to a person or to God, to some other vital being or process.

Level 1: Fortresses are made of stone. Fortresses ward off would-be attackers, enemies. Fortresses hold, and we are secure within them. Fortresses have been built in different ways in every civilization. Fortresses do not have to be physical only; we build fortresses with words and thoughts as well, such as in the construction of philosophies or institutions.

Level 1 (continued): God is strong. God saves people from destruction. God provides security. God is known in many ways by different peoples.

Young children can engage in these kinds of Level 1 thinking. Most people can.

But here is Level 2: "A mighty fortress *is* our God." The shorthand way of speaking (this poetic line) compresses all the Level 1 descriptive statements and causes something creatively different to happen.

It is the prayer of every sensitive church teacher that students will be able to move freely from Level 1 to Level 2 thinking. For it is only in doing this that we can create for ourselves the ultimate insight: We are the body of Christ.

We are the light of the world. We are the salt of the earth. We are the city on the hill that cannot be hidden. And on and on. Metaphors all, and we are *participants* in them, not just speakers. From the point of view of Christian education, it is the ultimate goal that we shall participate *in* rather than just talk about who we are in the sight of God.

The movement in conversation is progressive: comparing/contrasting; analogies in the form of simple similes; metaphors. And it appears that the way this progression moves along for most persons is directly related to the quality of daily conversation. We converse either with others or with ourselves, and we can enter into conversation with God. It is reflective give-and-take, in any case, and teachers have a splendid opportunity to nurture the art of conversation.

One of the original meanings of the English word "teacher" was "the index finger." A teacher is someone who points things out. But one does not point to things merely for the sake of pointing. It is in order to make a statement about those things, and to get the one who is observing (the student) to make a statement in reply. When David Elkind visited Dr. Piaget in Switzerland, they went for a walk to discuss ideas together. Dr. Elkind was struck by how many times his host would stop to point out a flower, a tree, or some other object of nature. His lifetime of observing phenomena impelled him to point the finger; he was teaching while conversing.

Conversation is initiated and continued. It has its culminating points, but there is a sense in which it never ends. For insofar as conversation activates learners (gets something going), it literally reverberates for a lifetime!

What About Memorization?

Some readers may wonder, why not place heavier emphasis upon requiring students to memorize things? Is it not a fact that we all need to have storehouses of memorized material, to serve us for a lifetime? And shouldn't teachers insist upon the acquisition of such stored memory?

These are fair questions. I am coming more and more to the conclusion that students *will* memorize things of importance if they perceive them to be worthy of their attention. At about grade 5 or so, young persons show a remarkable ability to assemble and remember literally thousands of facts. (They remember baseball statistics by the hundreds.) At this age level, they can master lists of names and books of Scripture and dates and places.

Memorizing seems to be done by internally created methods. It is not so much the programmed learning approach as it is the assembling of material in blocks and simply being able to call it up at random when needed.

To try to force memorization in earlier years is often disastrous and frustrating, for both teachers and students.

The point is that we memorize what is perceived to be *structurally important* by others as well as ourselves. A few years ago a group of junior highs committed to memory the entire Discourse of Jesus (Matt., chs. 5 to 7) and recited it in a public presentation. Why did they do it? Chiefly because an older woman whom they respected very much told them that it would change their lives if they learned it and thought about it. Something was activated; they wanted to learn this long passage and demonstrate that they had done it.[28]

Learning tasks like these, easily regarded as drudgery, become light burdens when we decide we *want* to accomplish them. Think, for instance, of the concert musician who memorizes long, complicated works to perform in public. What could possibly drive this person to do it except an inward desire born of the worth attached to the very act?

It all comes back, I believe, to the point where we began. It is in conversation, in the give-and-take with other individuals in the community, that we find our motives for memorization. Someone says something about the importance of being able to find one's way around in the Bible. It is a respected teacher, or a parent, or a much-loved friend. This sparks an inner resolve, and before long the learner puts into effect a system of personal "drilling" that results in a memorization job all neatly accomplished and ready for a lifetime of service.

In recent years I have discovered something about myself. I know dozens of hymns and can sing them all the way through without looking at the hymnal. How did that happen? I didn't make a conscious decision to memorize the stanzas, but through years of singing them in public worship, they have become part of me. In the same way, I can recite passages of Scripture that were never on my "memory verse" lists as a child at all. Through reading and study they have simply been impressed upon me so unforgettably as to be a part of my storehouse of memory. That's quite different from their having been laboriously "memorized" in a tedious effort.

The very fact that this kind of "absorption" happens to so many of us is a sound argument, I believe, for the adoption and steady use of an authorized version of the Bible. When translations and paraphrases proliferate as they have in the last two decades, the variations in texts are so great as to militate against memorization. To be memorized with facility, the text has to "stand still" enough to allow for it. The King James Version of the Bible is still a part of the memory structure of many thousands of persons. The Revised Standard Version holds that place for others. But not many people will find it easy to memorize the Scriptures if they hear varieties of translation read indiscriminately from week to week.

Many of us recite with deep appreciation the Nunc Dimittis, "Lord, now lettest thou thy servant depart in peace" (Luke 2:29). Recently I stood beside an older gentleman in a church where the minister read, "Lord, now let your servant go peacefully." My neighbor worshiper was outraged by this unforgivable trespass upon a thing of matchless beauty. A treasure of his youth had been tampered with, and to no good purpose!

The case I make, somewhat obliquely, is for a body, a corpus, of *structure* that becomes a part of our teaching/learning. These solid, remembered things that stay with us through all our days become the way stations as we talk about our faith, or sing about it. They contain the vital metaphors. They make it possible for the conversation of Christians to continue, generation to generation. We learn, and we pass on, "the language of Zion."

6 / Nurturing Depth
Through Language

Consider again the dialogue between Augustine and his son, at the beginning of Chapter 1. Is speaking in order to learn or in order to teach? Augustine's purpose is served by insisting that one speaks in order to teach, but we know that he is aware of the other side as well: one learns from speaking. It is in the use of language that we all give evidence of our having created points of view and structures of insight. Christian education is impossible without careful attention to language.

The behavioristic movement in education *is* concerned about language and learning. According to Skinnerian theory, it should be possible—strictly speaking—to impart to learners specific meanings for the words of our vocabulary; these meanings may be communicated by the S-R principle. Exemplars are given as stimuli, and the learner responds with naming. To teach "roundness," for instance, one would present a learner with a variety of round objects, calling attention to that characteristic. The name is "round." That response is reinforced until the word is committed to memory.

Similarly, according to the purely behavioral view, one may teach the rules of grammar by S-R procedure. Nouns, verbs, connectives, and modifiers are all identified and reinforced.

But is it really the case that a vocabulary plus the rules

of grammar will add up to an ability to form sentences and communicate? Computers can be taught these simple elements of language, but they do a poor job of speaking—and not solely because of the simplicity of our present programming.

Deeper than Rules

The behavioral theory of learning is simply inadequate to explain what happens in human communication. Something *deeper* is involved. Intelligent communication occurs through the use of words arranged in ways that simply do not exhibit all the rules of grammar. And sometimes sentences are spoken that are grammatically accurate and composed of familiar words; still, they make no sense whatsoever outside a contextual cue that is known to the speaker (and possibly listeners as well).

Here, for instance, is a statement that communicates:

"The eleven o'clock choir leaves just before the sermon."

The noun phrase "eleven o'clock choir" is intelligible to Protestant suburban worshipers. These large congregations usually have two or more services; the choir at eleven o'clock probably sang at nine or nine thirty, and its members return for the later service. The verb "leaves" conveys the idea of "leaves the church building," or "leaves the choir loft and exits from the church nave." The phrase "just before the sermon" includes the idea that the service of worship has distinct parts; a logical time for the choir to exit is just before the sermon, since the singers heard it at the earlier service and should not be expected to sit through it again.

Just observe how many bits and pieces of information, essential to the understanding of this sentence, are simply not grammatically present! They are below the surface of what the speaker is saying. And the listener *hears* below the surface, too. There is a depth to communication that is inexplicable by the strict application of the rules of sentence structure!

Now note this sentence:

"The piano was important because a fuse blew."

The structure is adequate; it has a subject, a predicate, and a dependent clause. Every word in it is a part of anyone's vocabulary. But what does it mean? The contextual *cue* is essential for its interpretation. Suppose we add the cue: "church organist." What begins to happen?

A mental picture emerges at once. The church organist was playing the organ, when an electrical fuse blew, making it impossible to continue. So the organist shifted to the piano. It was a good thing there happened to be a piano available; it's important to have a substitute instrument for use in public worship.

Again, something deeper is involved than mere vocabulary and rules of grammatical construction.

We may turn to the work of Noam Chomsky, gifted linguist and intellectual, for a theory that explains what is happening when we speak and listen.[29] He uses the word "deep" to suggest at least four elements at work in our human communication: *base components* (key ideas, concepts, that have become the basis of our culture), *deep structures* of grammar (in which we are free to think intuitively, without bothering to make everything perfectly logical and to fit it into a specific sequence), *transformations* (in which we open our mouths and form sentences), and a *surface structure* (typical of all daily discourse among persons).

And until we recognize that this complex activity is occurring all the day long, we do not fully appreciate the incredible depth of our language and of all that is involved in human speaking.

Chomsky's term for the deep structure and its consequential issue in intelligible speech is "generative grammar." He believes that language possesses the capacity to generate meaning. It is not so much that we create words and assign specific meanings to them. Words and their usage have a way of taking a kind of initiative of their own; they "generate" meanings. Language is, therefore, dynamic and constantly changing. Words create new meanings for themselves. From the "depths," the power of language rises to affect and change (transform) the ways in which we speak with one another.

Chomsky suggests that this character of human language is a genetic thing. We are literally born with the makeup out of which words take root and begin their generative processes.

He would be surprised to find himself in this book, for Chomsky has a view of theology and religion that is anything but dynamic. He thinks theology is devoted to saying the same thing over and over for the rest of one's life, and that there is nothing dynamic about it. Regrettably, he has not been exposed, apparently, to the excitement of discussions about God, people, and the world in a theological framework.

For it seems clear, to me at least, that the view of human beings as co-laborers with God, as creating individuals—a view that surely emerges from the Scriptures—is quite commensurate with Chomsky's ideas about language. "In the beginning was the Word . . . ," and that Word became known to us in the person of Jesus Christ (John, ch. 1). The "Word" is nothing static. Far from it, for it is the Word at work to "make all things new." Jesus Christ means different things to people in different eras of time. He is the same, yesterday, today, and forever. But he is also totally relevant and involved in the technological society just as he was in the agrarian, prescientific era.

Such is the case with all the words of our heritage. They take on their special meanings, generated and emerging from the depths. Chomsky speaks of "atom" as an example. When the ancient philosophers spoke of this word, they did not mean it in the same way we do; the word has simply changed while remaining the same. The generative (creative) process has been at work.

We could say the same for words such as "pastor" or "preacher" or "teacher." The meaning is different for each of these as time allows the generative power of each term to achieve its dynamic effect.

Nothing could be of greater consequence for teaching than a realization that something like Chomsky's generative grammar theory is indeed operative. We are involved, as teachers, in the exciting world of language. As activators, we can trigger what happens as learners reach into the depths and speak in their very own ways. We do not do the generating; it is a mysterious process made possible by the Creator. But it is our privilege to listen and to speak in order to learn and in order to teach.

So much hinges, I believe, on the relationship between deep structures and surface structures in thinking and speaking. In a society that lays such great store on daily barrages of words, via the media that inform, editorialize, comment, propagandize, and advertise, one can only wonder what kinds of base component are generating all this material.

W. Somerset Maugham, the British novelist-physician who was such a masterful storyteller and essayist, wrote about his own work in *The Summing Up*.[30] He spoke of times when he must exercise the most severe discipline to prevent his pen from taking over! There is a phenomenon familiar to writers and public speakers in which the words seem to "flow" almost effortlessly. Where are they coming from? The depths? Or the surface, as if from the pen itself, or just the lips? The words of many a facile speaker or writer, when analyzed, often turn out to be frothy and lacking in focus.

Similarly, many efforts to discuss or debate issues result in exchanges that seem never to resolve very much. Participants "talk past" one another without stopping reflectively to define terms and ponder meanings. This happens regularly in adult Bible study groups where persons "quote Scripture" to one another, often in the belief that this will nail down arguments decisively.

It is, of course, convenient for us to be able to locate lines of the Bible by citing chapter and verse. But there are times when one might wish no such device had ever been imposed upon the text. Pulling out a line, without regard to context, and reading or reciting it with an air of authority, has little to do with genuine thoughtfulness.

The problem here is essentially that the "deep structure" for Bible-quoting is often rooted chiefly in the concept of "Biblical authority" for its own sake. That is the base component: the Bible is the final and right arbiter for discussing issues. The concept of Biblical authority is very precious to me also, but there is something else that is deeper and from which all forms of authority (including that of Scripture) issue. The deeper Source is God in Jesus Christ. What matters is how the Scriptures, the Sacraments, the church, and our common life bear witness to Christ's creative rule over all.

If the concept of "Christ's rule (dominion)" is the foundation and source of our viewpoints, then discussion and debate, writing and speaking, all take on a different luster and exhibit qualities of a special dynamic: we struggle to listen carefully to one another; we search for answers to our dilemmas, together; we recognize that we shall never be fully satisfied with any human solution to our life issues. In short, we *struggle* to understand and also to speak in ways that others can follow. The struggle is not painful drudgery; it is a responsibility we accept as a privilege. For it pleases our Lord to be present among us and to work through us as he makes "all things new." A certain joy follows.

Christian educators, in their appointed role as interpreters, have a special obligation to be clear in speech and thought. They, above all, should be committed to the reflective use of language and to exploration for the ruling structures of discourse. It can be appalling to sit in meetings devoted to education and to listen to the surface structures of the participants' comments. Organizations, curricula, processes, ecclesiastical programs—all of these are denoted by initials: JED, NCC, CCD, NCEA, REA, and on and on. Our readiness to fall into such usage is highly suspect, in my opinion. We are too often obsessed with shorthand forms of speaking that leave our listeners agape. We convey the impression that it is our listeners' duty to "catch up" to us. Could it be our duty not to leave them behind?

The deep structures for Christian education, as well as for all other enterprises in the churches, are rooted in Jesus Christ, source and sustainer of our creative roles in the world. That is why we must come back again and again to the fundamental words: learning, teaching, community. And these fundamentals push us to consider verbs such as create, act, speak, listen. The jargon to which we all succumb is part of the transformation into a surface type of language and speech, and we cannot eliminate it from our daily discourse. But there is a necessary distinction we must make about the usages of jargon: It is one thing to use it because we understand so clearly what is truly important down below it. It is quite another to use jargon because we have nothing more at our fingertips or lips.

Generative Concepts

Committed Christian teachers are far from powerless in our sea of words! They can help deep structures of thought and speech to generate and grow.

For years now, I have observed how vital it is for both teachers and their students to pore over the key words that form the base for periods of study. These words provide the focus for class sessions and prevent both dullness and sameness. Every key word produces multiple possibilities for conceptual frameworks, and the mere recognition of this provides us with some measure of control, some possibility for disciplined thinking and speaking.

If I place a word on a chalkboard or overhead projector, everyone who sees it will immediately begin to place it into some kind of frame of reference. Some persons will be more analytical in their approach, quickly organizing lists of related terms and neatly labeling them as categories. Other persons will be more intuitive, allowing the word to call up a colorful universe of thought that is filled with feeling tones rather than neatly categorized images and terms. But whether we are more analytical or more intuitive at the outset is not the main issue. What matters truly is that the key word, the main constellation of ideas symbolized by it, is doing its "generative" work. It is attracting to itself, literally like a magnet, a wide variety of related materials. For each teacher, this process will issue in a unique pattern of thought.

Suppose the word is "edge."[31] I have used this one with hundreds of adults and youth. For some, it conjures images of sharpness and danger—knife, razor, or other instrument. For others (such as a clergy group with whom I worked for several days), it will signify precipice—being on the verge of vocational or personal disaster; nervous apprehension. Still others will think of "edge" as a word to be defined more precisely. One man, a space scientist, said that an edge is any point where two substances come together. Sometimes children will see edge as a happy word: "The cookies are on the edge where I can reach them."

Expressions such as "the edge of night," or "on the edge of a breakthrough," or "being on the growing edge" are sure to emerge in some groups.

Hardly anyone can recall a time when edge was not a part of everyday speech. The youngest children know the word ("Don't go too near the edge!"). It remains a vital part of our language; we need such a word.

This same process, applied to a word that has both con-

crete and abstract frames of reference, can be employed
with the words of our Christian heritage: worship, Shepherd, Savior, and countless others. What we discover, from
both teachers and their students, is the wide variety of
paths down which our thought processes travel. We observe what generative power these key words can have,
and how diverse the material that is generated. The psy-
chologist might call it "divergent class production," producing randomly the kinds of associated terms that can
later be classified and analyzed.

One also observes, on some occasions, how many of our
traditional "faith" words, such as love, grace, and hope,
are seen by students to be the *same* in meaning. Rich
understanding is missing, and the words of the tradition
are simply viewed as pointing to one another in a surface
type of circuit.

Our job is cut out for us. We are responsible, as teachers,
for assisting students to uncover additional material to
assemble creatively around each key term in the deep
structure of faith language. We do this by a variety of
strategies: telling stories, offering assignments in good
books, illustrating, role-playing, showing films, encourag-
ing interaction. Every technique known to us is useful if
we understand that we are seeking to magnify in importance, depth, and uniqueness each of the key terms of our
heritage. All of this is done not for the sake of linguistic
clarity alone; it is done to facilitate the work of Jesus
Christ. It is Christ's own person working in and through us,
knitting us together into a body that is intelligent and
deep, soulfully engaged in life and *saved* from the froth on
the surface of our culture. It is the same depth that is
needed in every generation.

Depth of language structure is *assumed* when we make
use of creeds and confessions in our churches. These brief
but carefully constructed statements of faith, arising in
particular historical contexts, are made possible as persons
acquire insight and are prepared to declare with certainty

what they believe and stand for. To recite a centuries-old creed in a liturgical setting is to acknowledge the worth of such declarations, and we do well to study carefully every word so that we can appropriate the meaning for ourselves in this present time. Teachers bear a responsibility for helping that process of inquiry to begin and continue.

Language itself changes, as we have already indicated. Any doubt that this is so is quickly dispelled when one looks at what has happened to words like "mankind" and "man," which were plainly used in a former time to mean "all persons" or "people." Some activists would insist that these words were subtly male-oriented even when we professed to use them generically for the whole of humankind. That may be, but it seems to me that one can be charitable and simply acknowledge that the meanings have changed. We can no longer look at "man" in any form and think both male and female; the language has changed, and man is now male. It will take a long time to accommodate the new usage with the former. Meanwhile, it is surely appropriate for us to be lenient with those who have spoken and written in the past, granting benefit of doubt and not accusing them inevitably of "sexism" each time we read "man" or "mankind" used in a generic sense.

The more important point for us to consider here, in connection with this current example of changing language, is the "deep structure" that generated the change. The concept of "human equality" or (for Christians) "equality before God" has been doing its generative work, and for this we may be deeply grateful. All races and ethnic groups are equal before God. All age groups are equal in the sight of God. And women and men are equal in the eyes of God. The movement toward making our language reflect, on the surface, this deep-down equality, is both logical and inevitable. The period of transformation will no doubt continue to yield some absurdities (such as "he or she" and "his or her" over and over!), but the end result will be worth it all. We shall be speaking with greater clarity and with loving concern.

All such matters are of great importance to teachers, for we are the ones who must bring them to the consciousness of learners. Teachers are necessarily concerned with the refinement of language and inquiry into meaning.

Faith and Words

It is, of course, more than a matter of niceties and proper usage. The commitment of a person to Jesus Christ involves acquiring a faith stance that is inseparable from words that are used to describe it. Having the right words, each invested with meaning personally appropriated and lived out, helps to shape what we are. We will be what we call ourselves, and we will act as we define what is appropriate, relying on the grace of God to forgive us when we fail to live up to our high calling. Let us consider some word combinations that illustrate this generative power of language to assist in our Christian "formation."

1. *Worship as a response.* Teachers and students in the Christian tradition acknowledge the obligation and necessity to be worshipers. All worship, private and corporate, has the potential of becoming perfunctory performance of ritual acts. But when the word is linked with "response," something significant begins to happen. We begin to see worship as a way of acknowledging what God has done for us and what God continues to accomplish for our sakes. To pray, to sing, to ponder Scripture, to receive the Sacraments—all of these are acts in which we make the only appropriate move that can be made by grateful, forgiven sinners. Who among us can ever say we have done enough to acknowledge our gratitude to God?

Teachers have many opportunities to inculcate this linking of "worship" with "response." Times for prayer and singing, in class sessions, should correspond to those culminating moments when students have found out something significant for their lives; the next appropriate move is to say thank you to God who made this possible. Worship is essentially our bowing down to offer ourselves totally to the Creator who sustains us and works through us.

If one removes the idea of "responding" from the concept of worship, then an entirely different mode of being will ensue. To make a conscious effort to imbue our students with the deep structure of "worship as response" is a worthy educational goal; it makes a difference not only for individual worshipers but also for the entire Christian community.

2. *Human relationships as covenants.* Every teacher will readily grant that our relationships with one another as persons are of paramount concern in a Christian community. Teacher-student, boy-girl, parent-child, husband-wife—these are only a few of the relationships that receive attention in our curricula. We care about sensitive attention to the needs of one another across all these hyphens!

But if we see the relationships as *bound* by a "covenant," something quite different is involved. Parties to a covenant recognize realistically that there will be times when relationships are not all rosy and pleasant. There will be disagreements and misunderstandings, hurt feelings and need for reconciliation. Such healing and restoration is possible if both parties honor the covenant made between them. Parents have a covenantal duty to bring up their children and provide for their needs in every sphere; children have a covenantal duty to respect and honor their caring parents. Husbands and wives are covenantally related in sickness and in health, in joy and in sorrow, in plenty and in want. When the qualities of "romance" seem to be absent from a marriage, something deeper and more compelling is there to bring both husband and wife back into joyful relationship; it is the concept of marriage as a covenant, as something that requires work and vigilance if it is to remain strong and to grow with the passing of the years.

The covenant idea is at the very heart of the Judeo-

Christian tradition. It is the same word as "testament," and we look upon all our relationships as aspects of the covenant that God has made with all who turn to Jesus Christ in faith.

Again, if the word "covenant" is removed, something quite different will follow. It is the power of this word, taught and constantly reexamined, that offers a new dimension to human relationships. The deep structure of the expression "binding in covenant" will inform and shape the lives of people. Teachers who believe that will make every effort to honor the concept in their classrooms.

I was visiting in a village church where I would be working with a group of church teachers. In a few moments I would be teaching a practice class, with observers. My students were boys and girls of grades 5–6. A girl in the group said to me: "Our teacher here at this church hardly ever comes to class on time. Sometimes she doesn't even come, so we just sit in this room and don't have anything to do on those days." Inwardly, I was asking myself what this would say about the teacher's view of her covenantal role. And what sort of view was being communicated to the students in that church? Sometimes these simple episodes expose our deep structures for what they really are. I would imagine the teacher of these boys and girls harbored the down-deep view that teaching doesn't really matter all that much. The covenantal aspect of it was missing, for her.

Promises made and kept, agreements negotiated and honored, solemn affirmations encouraged and respected, resolutions offered and adopted—all these kinds of human commitment are present in the church classroom or in any community of Christians. They are ways of saying: "We are a covenant people. All relationships under God are part of the covenant."

3. *Work as service.* Work is both a divine and a human activity. God worked in the Creation, and God rested from

the labor of it. We are workers—in the God-given task of stewardship over all that is in the world, and in the production of all the fruits of civilization. Teachers and students see themselves as workers, laborers in the vineyard of the Lord.

So much has been said in our time about the meaninglessness of human labor in the technological society. We have been told we are anonymous ciphers in the process. But this has been much overdrawn, in my opinion. With a bit of instruction and a chance for reflection, most persons who are engaged in routine tasks can see how their work, however mundane it may seem, is an essential part of a larger process. How each job, each task, is performed is of vital importance to the whole. Work is a service to self, to others, and to the larger community (even the whole world).

For this very reason Christians care about the unemployment rate and the high rate of forced idleness among young people. To be unemployed, not to have one's potential challenged and utilized, is to be deprived of an opportunity to serve worthily in the field of daily labor.

In the office where I work, we had a young man who came to us out of college. He had majored in physics at the university, and he was a good student. In a few months he would be leaving for officer training in the Air Force. It wasn't long until we observed that Randy Baareman was an exceptional person. His job with us was that of a mailing clerk, but he made it much more—on his own. He came early and left late. He thought of new ways to do each day's assigned tasks. He answered the telephone with utmost courtesy and helpfulness. He gave himself selflessly to what could have been "just a job." He refused to "mark time"; instead, he looked upon his work as a service.

Randy learned this point of view about work. It was not just an accident. Where did he get this concept of serving? It came from his active participation in a Christian family and a Christian church. There is no other way to account for his special qualities. He is a servant of God in his daily work.

Teachers who work hard at their teaching, who make a sincere effort to let their classrooms reflect their concept of service, and who speak overtly to their students about all work as a form of service to God are helping to build a deep structure of language and action: "Work is serving."

If you take away the "service" concept from work, the consequences are immediately observable. Work becomes a humdrum activity, often performed without imagination and even grudgingly. We can see this happening all around us, in the decline of skills and in the evident lack of personal joy in daily tasks.

Obviously, one cannot change all of this simply by saying to another, "Work is serving." But Christians gather week after week to consider how they shall respond as covenant people to the great work of Jesus Christ in their behalf. It is surely possible to stress and demonstrate that one form of response is to make our jobs, however menial, into acts of service to others whom God has set in community with us. The service concept becomes a motivating force. And it is partly because of the generative power of these two words linked in the consciousness of persons: "work" with "service."

The Power of Language

Perhaps these three examples are adequate to illustrate what I have been saying. Language in combination with acts of commitment has power to shape what we are. It is not a reflexive, S-R kind of shaping. It is a generative process that starts with a linkage in terms and a vision of how that linking will be forever relevant. One cannot speak or think about this process without using the word "deep." It is no surface matter when a deeply seated language motif informs and profoundly affects daily human activity.

This is one reason why schools and classrooms can be so important. They provide a quiet place, removed from the maelstrom, where teachers and students can speak and listen. Here is where language-in-relation-to-being can become a consciously examined aspect of our living.

Think of some teacher who meant much to you. You will remember mannerisms, appearance, possibly little episodes that demonstrated kindness or consideration. But it is highly likely that you will also recall something that teacher *said* which you have never forgotten. I remember a teacher who said, "Half an education is knowing where to find things." Another teacher: "Carelessness is the supreme conceit." Another: "If we make fewer rules, fewer will be broken."

These recalled "sayings" of favorite teachers are incorporated in some way into our own world view, our own way of considering self and personal responsibility. We pass them along to others. When pressed to offer some word of counsel, we surprise ourselves by recalling and repeating what someone once said to us in such a time— and often it is a word from someone who was in a teaching role.

I realize I am in danger of being misunderstood. I do not mean to say that teaching is only speaking, or that the right words incorporated into lessons will make for surefire results in students' lives. But I do seek to make a case for the role of language in our makeup as persons. We are moved to act in certain ways, and the power of dominant word combinations must not be minimized.

Recently I met a man who had been going to church all his life. But within months of our meeting, something had begun to happen to him. He reported: "I never understood before what all those things said and done in church meant. Suddenly, it is coming clear. I can't seem to find out enough these days, my faith in Christ has come to mean so much to me!"

A surface structure had at last been connected, for him,

to a meaningful deep structure. The words of faith were viscerally important in a way they had not been before. We have all had that experience, in one degree or another; a word or phrase, long dormant, comes into consciousness in a new way—and it seems to have a power of its own to cause us to remark: "This is important! Why didn't I see this before?"

Teachers and students work with the surface matters. But it is surely possible to get to the deeper levels as well. Every good classroom situation will include those moments when someone indicates an "Aha!" Ideas previously encountered have fallen into place in a new way so that a student (or teacher) can say something differently—articulate a concept with a depth previously unattainable. Words are integral to the process. Even where the event is supposedly nonverbal, there comes a time when the learner will seek to put into words what was deeply felt or apprehended.

The most effective teachers, conscious of these phenomena of which I have been speaking, will have a special respect for the power of words. They will avoid offering closed definitions, especially of the great words of the faith. The preferred way of defining the formulas for stating relationships among terms, the memorized synonym lists—all of these have to be reconsidered when one is speaking of deep language structure.

Teachers first must have their own clear grasp of the "sweep" of our faith history—of the covenants established by God with a chosen people, of the wanderings and returnings of Israel, of the new covenant in Christ and the hope we all enjoy as forgiven and accepted sinners, received and loved by the very Creator of life. This sense of identity as a person in the new community through which God is working out a purpose and making all things new becomes the raison d'être for the teacher's work with students. Out of that integrated understanding of who we are, we teachers can be present among our students in a meaningful way, assisting them to explore, examine, inquire, in order to grasp that same sweep of history that has caught us up and will not let us go.

We are then freed, by our own grasp of our identity in Christ, to engage our students in a quest. The quest is for understanding, for an empowering language that both informs and generates. Words we study are seen in the context of our history as a people of God. Key terms and phrases are continually reexamined for new dimensions.

Consider, for instance, the word "sacrifice," from which we derive all aspects of "sacerdotal" understanding. We can trace that word through the Old Testament and into the New. We can see in a special way what it was that Jesus Christ offered, as the "perfect sacrifice." And we can see how the word informs our worship, especially the Lord's Supper. It is a word that is indispensable to understanding a Christian's view of human service. We willingly sacrifice our own comfort and satisfaction, our own need for indulgence, in order to satisfy the needs of others. We do it without grudging because we care. We are responding, through our own life-style of sacrificial giving and serving, to the supreme sacrifice made in our behalf.

This is not something that is taught in a day. But it is gradually communicated and established within the psyches of participants in Christian community. It is one of those focal terms without which our ability to express what it means to be Christian would be greatly impoverished.

How does a teacher assist in building a deep structure for the word "sacrifice" in the vocabularies of students? Partly by asking them to look up the word in the dictionary. Partly by research assignments in Scripture. Partly by telling stories about sacrificial living. Partly by the use of meaningful liturgy that includes the concept.

But mostly, the teacher's communication of the meaning of "sacrificial" will be demonstrated through the linking of the articulated word with a life-style that is consistent with the word. Is this teacher a person who freely gives time for the sake of individuals in the class? Is this teacher someone who freely shares talents and possessions for the sake of others? There needs to be this commensurate aspect, this "squaring" of what the teacher says with what the teacher does, this evidence that the surface and the deep structures are "in touch" for him or her.

Anchoring Pins

Then, too, the words and phrases of our faith—in addition to being seen as relevant to the total sweep of faith history—must also be seen as open to continued exploration and investigation. They are introduced as "stakes" or "anchoring points" for a growing process, a lifelong pilgrimage of searching and building up accrued meaning.

It's always troubling, for me, when I have completed a forty-five minute practice class with a group of students, to hear one of the adult observers say: "But you didn't 'cover' everything. You didn't answer all the questions. You didn't tie things up."

For that is exactly what I don't want to do—to "tie things up." It is so important in the process of activating to leave room for seeds to sprout, to take root, and to grow. These are the best indications that such room is being allowed:

Teacher: That's a good beginning. You'll find lots more to wonder about in this book.

Teacher: We haven't discovered very much yet in our research. There's plenty to "dig for" next time.

Teacher: Between now and the next time we meet, see what you can find out about . . .

We must achieve just the right balance—enough defining and establishing of meanings for words and phrases to provide anchoring points for our students; we do *not* leave them adrift. But we don't anchor the boat so firmly that there is no more movement, no more journeying to another port of insight. Things have to be left open for further investigation, further routes of inquiry.

This combination of the anchoring idea with the aspect of openness in our teaching calls for our thinking through more clearly than we have in the past just which concepts are key (cardinal, central). Whitehead was right when he said we should teach fewer subjects, and I am right when I insist that certain identifiable concepts become the motifs for our study in the church. If we spread ourselves so thin as to attack hundreds of words and phrases every few hours in our classes, we then persist in making our teaching only a matter of surface structure.

The concepts we choose (and they may be different in differing Christian traditions) will collectively become the deep structure for our language of faith. It is then a matter of nurturing our students by providing a wide variety of experiences that supply more and more flesh on the skeleton, more and more accrued insight into the power of faith language to shape who we are and how we act. But all is to no avail without the life-giving presence of *the* Word, Jesus Christ, who is there in the process.

EDUCATING / Work
of Community

And his gifts were that some
should be apostles, some
prophets, some evangelists, some
pastors and teachers, . . . for the
work of ministry, for building up
the body of Christ.

Eph. 4:11–12

7 / Searching for a Focus

Learning is an act of creating. Teaching is a process of activating. What, then, do we do with the word "education"? There is no clear consensus regarding the nature of education, and the term "Christian education" has proved problematic for many years. I will avoid sifting through history and rehashing issues long under debate about this term. I propose instead to sketch some dilemmas and offer a few directions I believe would be profitable for the churches.

We must begin by considering whether education is a general or specific term. Lawrence Cremin, well-respected authority in the field, regards education as a term designating specific endeavors, planned and carried out with a deliberate purpose. That is to say, schools seek to educate. They plan curricula, employ faculties, and proceed about their business of educating. Education is also undertaken by the public media (newspapers, radio, television), and by other groups in our society such as political parties, volunteer agencies, industries, the military.

Cremin acknowledges that people learn things, and appropriate them in their lives, quite apart from all these educational efforts. All the experiences of human beings have potential for producing learning. Learning is the general term; education is specific.[32]

But one can make a case for another frequently heard position: that learning is specific and education general.

143

Such a viewpoint holds that we plan for learning to happen, and we design activities to make it possible. Education, on the other hand, is the totality of human experience. Everything that happens to us in the course of our lifetimes has an educative effect. We are educated through the process of living.

Christian educators have tended to opt for the latter view. They hold that education is a term embracing the whole of what happens to us in our pilgrimage. As it is affected by Christian values or Christian emphases, explicit or subtle, it can be called Christian education. It is hard to pin down the Christian educationist; everything is ultimately "Christian education," and we should endeavor to maintain this global view, we are so often told.

It is not surprising that Christian education should have abandoned its focus on a specific domain of activity. This has been the trend in the churches for quite some time, and I can cite several examples.

Consider, for instance, the word "mission." At one time that term was fairly clear. A mission was an assignment that was quite specific. We had foreign missions, and we had local and national missions. We knew what that meant. Then, in a burst of theological enthusiasm during the 1950's, practically everything under the sun became "mission." Our very existence is mission, we were told. That is true, in a sense, but the expansion of the word to embrace so much—and the repeated emphasis on its general nature—led to the collapse of the term. The word could not stand under so much weight. We were tripping over ourselves trying to make everything said or done fit into "mission." My own denomination changed its Board of Foreign Missions to Commission on Ecumenical Mission and Relations. It was a redundant term, since "commission" is so closely related to "mission"; indeed, it contains the same concept. One had to explain the name over and over again, and the best way to explain was simply to say, "It's our former Board of Foreign Missions." The effort to embrace so much, to be so general, was self-defeating. A specific thrust of the church—mission work in other countries—was made less pointed and urgent, it seemed to me.

Then there was the word "stewardship." In simpler times, we seemed to know that this meant giving the necessary money and supplies to keep the work of the church moving eagerly forward. But again, in a frenzy of explanatory papers, stewardship was redefined to mean the totality of our living in this world. Everything we do was said to be stewardship. Well, that is true in the grandest sense. But then "stewardship" became somewhat useless as a term; it meant the same thing as mission. Indeed, departments of stewardship, with clear-cut roles to play in the churches, became divisions of "mission interpretation." Again, lots more explaining had to be done, for a word had become so general that it collapsed under the weight given to it.

One more example: "evangelism." It seemed plain enough at one time that evangelism meant the conscious act of asking people to commit their lives to Jesus Christ and to take their places in his body. But that word, too, became foggy. Persons were saying that everything Christians do in the world is evangelism; we proclaim the good news by our entire lives. True enough, in an ultimate sense. But the word collapsed under its burden. Before long, departments of evangelism very nearly died away. The specificity of an important task had given way to a generalization.

Mission, stewardship, and evangelism are all Biblical and churchly words, and we cannot escape their importance. They are always capable of resuscitation!

Education Goes Global

The word "education" is not Biblical, and it is not a part of the major portion of the church's history. It is a new discipline that was preoccupied at first with the improvement of teaching and learning in school types of settings under the auspices of the churches. It was only within the first half of this century that the Boards of Sabbath School Work or Sunday School Boards began to change their names to Boards of Christian Education. A thing tends to be what you name it. A term like "Christian education," even more than others, invited the process of generalizing. The whole universe could come under such an umbrella.

A new world was revealed to me when I became a part of a national Christian education staff. At that time about forty of us were classified as "staff." Within a few years we were heading toward one hundred, for we had taken on responsibility for the following: education for mission, education for stewardship, education for evangelism, education for social action. And there were many practical subdivisions: education for youth camping, education for church officers, and the like. The division of higher education included colleges, youth movements, vocational guidance, faculty development, scholarship programs, and other functions. Seminaries came under a council on theological education—probably one of the most specific agencies of all.

In the seminaries, practical courses had at one time focused on topics such as how to do Sunday school work or how to lead youth groups. These gave way to departments of Christian education that sought to relate the word "education" to the church's total life. This necessitated philosophical, psychological, sociological, and theological inquiry. Christian education became interdisciplinary, highly global in scope.

Within the last two decades I have observed a considerable number of Christian educators who have, in effect, written and lectured themselves right out of their jobs. They left their field behind in order to become specialists in other more manageable (or, for them, more exciting) areas of study: social psychology, organizational develop-

ment, moral education, and so forth. Departments of
Christian education are seldom vibrant; they are addenda,
often with muted voices.

It was possibly inevitable. The trend toward generalization, the turning away from the specific and identifiable,
has caused "education" to flounder in the churches.

I must add here a recollection of one refreshing moment. In the early 1960's I was a visitor in Richmond,
Virginia, to observe the Presbyterian Church U.S. staff at
work on their new Covenant Life Curriculum materials.
Presiding over a huge stack of manuscripts and an incredible schedule of deadlines sat a remarkable woman, Dr.
Rachel Henderlite. Someone in our group asked her what
she was going to *do* about some far-reaching educational
issue of the day; I don't recall just which issue it was. She
replied: "Nothing. That's not my responsibility. I'm here
to see that this curriculum gets produced and into the
hands of the teachers." She was the first person I had
heard in years who would disclaim responsibility for the
entire universe of Christian education. It was a disease.
We all felt responsible for everything that went on in the
whole world, or so it seemed.

Perhaps the time will shortly come when we seek to
make all these terms we use in the church more specific,
when we recover some sense of "focus." To be clear about
the range of meaning for a given, time-honored word is
not to diminish its greatness; indeed, each word deserves
the privilege of standing specifically for something.

Gabriel Moran, outstanding Roman Catholic writer in
the field, defined education more recently as "the improvement of human life through the devising of structures for learning." One might expect that he would then
be more specific about the "structures" for which educators and teachers should be particularly responsible. Instead, he opts for the approach of generalization: "Almost
anything can function as an educational instrument if it
serves this aim of human development." In short, then,

everything the church does that is aimed at improving human life is education. Moran concludes that the church educates by "being itself."[33]

He has important things to say about the attitudes of church leaders toward the people, about the nature of parish life, and about the need for a sense of community among all persons who call themselves Christian. But in the end one can only wonder: Would these same generalizations, these same important appeals, not be just as appropriate in a discussion of "evangelism," "stewardship," "mission," or even "faith" itself? The zeal to be inclusive, to reach for the grand design that leaves nothing out, leaves us with a sense of puzzlement. Is it possible to carve out a respectable and worthy field of labor for teachers and educators? Or must we always be responsible for burdens larger than we can bear?

Disillusioned with Institutions

We got into this dilemma, I believe, because of a wave of disillusionment with institutions. Everyone knowledgeable about the history of the churches in the last quarter of a century will recall the agonizing reappraisals of the "institutional church." One could point to the shortcomings and lack of prophetic witness on the part of appointed and elected leaders. Or one could be harshly critical of the persons who sat in the "comfortable pew" and were supposedly insensitive to the pain and injustice in the world. One could also despair over the spending of money and energy for what Peter Berger called "the noise of solemn assemblies." The church was tattered to shreds in the 1960's. The institution had failed, and its renewal was doubted.

Still, there was something called "church"—the gathering of the faithful to bear witness to Christ as Lord. A faithful remnant battled for an end to racial segregation, for peace and justice in the world, and for sensitivity to human need. We are still too close to the turbulent years to assess it all properly. Was it really true that the "institution" had been so ineffective and impotent? Or was it indeed the institution that brought up its sons and daughters to speak out at last?

The same questions could be asked about schools, colleges, and universities. It was a popular thing for young Christians to invoke the names of Ivan Illich and Paulo Freire in a wave of critical unrest with regard to schooling. Incensed by alignments of the educational establishment with status quo thinking, enraged by curricula that seemed out of tune with the issues of the day, thousands of sensitive persons—joined by militant anarchists, in some cases—set out to attack the institution of the school. Schooling was said to be the institutionally limiting opponent of true education. Liberation of the oppressed could not come until this model had been exposed for its failures.

In a quite proper zeal for social justice, students became aggressive. They tried to cripple or destroy their universities. In so doing, they discovered that these institutions were very fragile. Even a Harvard *could* be destroyed, they observed. It is to the credit of that generation of youth that they did, in the end, recoil from their own power. The truth was unmistakable: there is something essentially good about gatherings of persons in "seats of learning." The word "school" is battered and scarred, but it is still alive. *If schools were destroyed, they would have to be reinvented.*

Curiously, when Americans went to Mexico to see how Illich was living out his social philosophy, one of the most tangible aspects of his work was language study. Classes were organized, and people sat out of doors in groups, following their instructors' directions as they learned to speak Spanish. One young professor of education noted that it might have been more comfortable for such an undertaking if there had been some modest classrooms available! The school had been reinvented as the necessity arose for the teaching of language classes.

Among the Christian educators who took up the de-schooling theme with intentional seriousness was John Westerhoff. He still speaks occasionally of our real problem as having fallen for the "schooling-instructional paradigm." He grows impatient (as we all do!) with humdrum schools. He calls for a new seriousness about education. It will come about, he believes, when we recognize the bankruptcy of the school and begin to preoccupy ourselves with the word "faith." He sees schooling as antithetical to inspiration, as somehow a deterrent to "faith development."[34]

Sometimes I become quite provoked about this whole issue. Westerhoff has inveighed against schools with the best of intentions. He wants something better than he sees issuing from the organized approaches to teaching and learning in the churches. But I am quite certain that these schools, if they could be destroyed by articulate criticism, would in due time be resurrected. They are not the monstrous deterrents to faith development that he supposes; they are simply the fragile efforts of Christians to carry out the commission, "Go, teach."

During the years when Westerhoff was treating this issue with his best punches, I was plugging away at the same problem by working within the schools. I had to find out for myself whether there was a redemptive role to be played by organized classes for the purpose of exploring our heritage and our mission as Christians. In laboratory settings throughout the country, in every conceivable sort of socioeconomic setting, I was engaging in a ministry of teaching. I found none of the sterility and impotence that was supposed to be present in such efforts. Instead, I found human beings with God-given creativity, ready to be loved and taught. It is a long story, but it would become a biography of my own "faith development."

This excursion into the "schooling" issue is essential to

show that the Christian education establishment suffered an era of disillusionment with all institutions. The church itself, the colleges, the universities, even the struggling Sunday school, were not spared. In understandable frustration, Christian educators became confused about their role in the church. The response of many was to generalize to the point of speaking about education as simply the total work of the church. All such broad definitions, however idealistically motivated, have in the end served to weaken, depress, and obliterate the simple ministries of teaching that are so very worthy of our time and effort and careful devotion.

Surely I do not believe that schools are the only place where teaching and learning occur. Homes are more important than schools. Other vital groupings of human beings have a strong influence upon us all—work places, social organizations, even gangs.

But still there is a vital role for something called the "school." It is the ever-present, smoldering backlog that makes possible the preservation of our tradition. Gatherings of teachers and learners in designated places—that is what schools are. These gatherings are the logical accompaniment of a people serious about listening to the Word of God and asking what it means for each generation.

We believe that people should be literate in order to live with the content of our faith. In schools we work to preserve and develop literacy.

We believe that people should engage in debate and dialectic, under the tutelage of learned persons. Our reading of the apostle Paul surely launches us toward that view of the Christian's duty in a world that is always at odds with the gospel. In schools we work to enhance the quality and incisiveness of that debate, that intellectual struggle.

Our Christian heritage, like the heritage of Judaism, links the pursuit of learning with responsible service to God. We survey the history of human gatherings for that purpose, and the lamp flickers often. But it never goes out entirely. It would be the *supreme irony* if, in our own time, the lamp were extinguished not by the forces that work against the gospel but by the Christian educators who were impatient to do something "better"!

The realistic course, it seems to me, is to work our way back to specifics again. The first of these specifics might be to recognize that gatherings of people for teaching and learning are necessary and at all times appropriate. There is no need to apologize for the word "school" in connection with such a gathering; we can allow that schools have been dismal places (sometimes) and that people who work in schools can be insensitive and without adequate vision (sometimes). But the same thing can be said, critically, of all human efforts "to improve life."

Schools are a *convenient locus* for a ministry of teaching that energizes and affects all other scenes of teaching and learning. Schooling is a positive term if we turn our attention to its potential for activating persons. It is a positive term if we consider how it can be the scene of the creativity we call learning.

Schooling can be joyful and fulfilling if it is seen as an instrument of the Creator. Jesus Christ can be present in a school to live within and work through teachers and learners, as they "make something" out of life in a collaborative effort. Jesus Christ can offer forgiveness and acceptance, and a direction for living, in a classroom just as well as anywhere else. It is what teachers and learners do in schools that should be our proper area of concern. A ministry of teaching worthy of Christ *can* happen there. And from the sparks ignited in such settings, lives can be affected in every domain of life. Christ who makes "all things new" calls us to school for the fulfillment of our role in creation. School need not stifle initiative or snuff out the breath of spirituality. On the contrary, it can do just the opposite—nurture initiative and inspire deeply.

Education Gives Life Direction

Let us come back to the term "education." I do not imagine for a moment that it can be eliminated from our churches' vocabulary. We need to find a worthy way of speaking about it, a definition that will not overburden it. Is there a way to think of education as *specific*, inasmuch as we have seen the difficulties arising from regarding it as such a general enterprise? Can education take on a form so that we can at least speak about it without being tongue-tied?

Perhaps a way to begin would be to note that a person is educated when he or she has taken a certain direction in life. One is educated to be a doctor, a nurse, a lawyer, a priest. Or one is educated to be a Christian, a Jew, or a Moslem. Or one is educated to be a liberal or conservative Democrat, a conservative or liberal Republican, or a Socialist. Or one is educated to be an exemplary American citizen, a loyal British subject, a French-Canadian patriot. We are reared and launched in a direction, partly of our own choosing but partly as a result of circumstance. Education is, ultimately, the name we give to this direction-taking process.

Education is pathfinding. We make certain moves that determine our next steps. And out of the experience of finding our way, we take on certain characteristics that mark us out with specified identity.

I think back to my own high school graduating class—a very small class in a rural school. As it happened, I was the only one who went to college. Others got jobs and married earlier than I did. We went our various ways, and I know only one of them now; the others are presumably still living, but I do not know where.

So one would have to say that each of us in that class was educated differently beyond high school. We acquired quite varied points of view about life, work, and family.

The simple reason for this is that each of us became part of new and separate *communities.*

The communities we find ourselves in profoundly affect the directions we take. College is a community; graduate school is a community; work places are communities; recreational groups are communities.

Education is a collective enterprise undertaken by community members: parents, teachers, peers, political leaders, writers and speakers, and many others. Certain types of communities tend to produce certain characteristics in their members. Our ethnic consciousness, heightened in recent years, is a frank acknowledgment that such community-related identity is important to us. We are hungry to know and appreciate our roots, and we want to be faithful to the best that comes to us from our heritages. We seek to discover the mind-set, the spirit, of our individual identities as community members.

Christian education, if we use that term, is the work of community. It is the quite specific *thrust* or direction consciously adopted and displayed by a group of Christians. It is unabashedly local and parochial while cognizant of the larger world scene. It is definable, visible, and capable of being achieved. Christian education is not the same in rural settings as in suburban or urban; every community has its own characteristics and must be sensitive to those special needs and qualities that give it a distinctive flavor. The apostle Paul, in his journeys to cities of widely differing cultures, never once suggested that Christians would take on a homogenized look. One may assume that he accepted the differences and sought to inspire churches indigenous to each location. It is this attention to the gathered community that characterizes Christian education and makes it quite specific. I am told by persons who were present at Vatican II, which has so profoundly affected all of Christendom, that one of the most impressive aspects of that gathering was the realization that the Roman Catholic communion is not monolithic; it is quite diverse, and its vitality in the world is due to that diversity maintained in a spirit of unity.

One might speak of the "flavor" of denominational groups: stress on given concepts of deeply held convictions. For instance, the Society of Friends, although small in numbers, retains its emphasis on inner light and the efficacy of silence. Baptists retain a distinctive simplicity in worship; United Methodists are still known as a singing church. These are specific qualities of identifiable communities of Christians that do not survive simply by happenstance. There is an educative effort to perpetuate what is distinctive in each of them. But I am not referring merely to denominational differences.

Life-oriented Issues

Christian education is the work of any discernible gathering of Christians who are regularly together in community. The task is to supply a point of orientation around which the teaching and learning take place. One learns in community what is of immediately vital importance in that place. And one teaches in community what is considered most needful for that time and location.

Consider, for instance, these kinds of concerns that have every reason to be the concern of Christian communities, and hence of Christian education/educators:

1. *Sex roles and marriage.* It is entirely appropriate for the Christian community to work on the matter of what it means to be male and female, and to be supportive and concerned about the single persons and widowed as well as those who marry. Attention to our sex roles and how they are handled is not something obliquely or peripherally considered in a church; they are such primary aspects of our daily life that they should be wholesomely discussed and pondered. Christian education works for definitions of health and wholeness in the field of human sexuality, in the precious bond of marriage, and in the living out of

one's role as man or woman in modern society.

It has been suggested for years now that these areas are marked by "confusion" in contemporary thought. If that is so, then Christian educators have their work cut out for them. Clarity can come if communities labor prayerfully to achieve better insight.

2. *Child-rearing and family life.* If each set of parents, each family, must be left on its own to work out life-styles and codes of behavior, the community is broken and divided. Children and youth are left confused. What is an appropriate bedtime for youngsters? When and where may children congregate to play, and for how long? What are the community standards? One does not have to resort to legalisms and undue restriction in order to arrive at accepted norms if a sense of community is present, and if educative effort has been devoted to building Christian family life.

Christian educators will do well to help parents get together to discuss all these matters and to form points of view that are intelligently arrived at—permeated with the freedom of the gospel, yet strong enough to withstand the temptations of "anything goes."

3. *Citizenship and leadership.* Who shoulders the burdens of leadership in a democratic society? How are such burdens shared? And who protects the public from possible abuses of power on the part of chosen leaders? All such matters are the appropriate concern of Christian communities, at their local level. Far from being "outside the bounds" of church, the matter of citizenship is a primary issue. In an increasingly energy-conscious nation, will Christians ignore the 55 mile an hour speed limit? What kinds of covenants of citizenship would Christians be able to make, setting aside their partisan political loyalties?

Christian educators have plenty to work on here, and it is all specific and local. There is nothing vague about it.

4. *Diet, drugs, and health.* Our Jewish ancestors were deeply concerned about what was appropriate for eating.

Christians in some communities have shown deep interest in dietary regulations. Now that we know so much more about the nature of nutrition, is it not the concern of Christians to see that community practice is commensurate with the best health habits?

When members of the community are alcoholics or addicted to other drugs, including tobacco, this is of paramount concern. Where are the best treatment centers? How does one get a person who needs treatment admitted to a good hospital or center?

If obesity is known to cause health problems and economic dislocation for families, then is it not a community responsibility to help persons lose weight? (I have been appalled at the number of grossly overweight students in theological seminaries. They should absolutely be required to do something about it, in my opinion.)

It is no denial of Christian freedom to express real concern about diet and health care in our time. This is something totally specific to which Christian educators can give their attention.

5. *Clothing and shelter.* The quality of housing and the adequacy of clothing for all members of the community are topics for concern in most areas. What can be done to provide shelter at prices people can afford, for so long as they live? And where can the best values be obtained for the purchase of clothing? What are the best methods of caring for clothing made of the various fabrics?

These are nitty-gritty matters, as we say. But they are legitimately a part of the educational concern in any community. Christians care about them!

6. *Seedtime, harvest, and animal husbandry.* How to plant and grow crops to provide for the well-being of people; how to conserve the soil and make it most productive; how to breed, raise, and market animals; how to assure that the environment is preserved and not polluted —all of these are community concerns about which Christians will have specific insights based on their understand-

ing of the role of humankind in the natural world.

Christian educators keep their eyes and ears open to what is happening to the earth around them. The specifics of each spring's plantings and each autumn's harvests should not elude us, for these are related to what we believe about God and Providence.

7. *Finances.* Where people get their money and how they spend it is important to the Christian educator, and not because we are charged with raising money to support religious causes. Our concern is to deal with the values that are represented in acquiring wealth and distributing resources. These values are communicated through community effort to face the issues of selfishness and generosity, of frugality and extravagance, of labor and sloth. All these fundamental issues, deeply related to the quality of a Christian's life, are bound up with the everyday financial decisions we make. Sensitivity to our God-given responsibility to care for the financial needs of community members is not something that just happens. It requires specific, educative effort.

8. *Health care.* What can we say about the quality of care given to the sick and the aging in our communities? People have to learn not only how to evaluate the health-care professions and facilities but also how to do some of this caring themselves. When is it most appropriate to place aging parents in nursing homes? When might it be better not to consider such a step?

These are not matters to be left only to the doctors and nurses. Every member of the community needs to talk them through and to form judgments based on the best possible insight born of Christian conviction and concern.

Christian educators need to be right in the middle of the health-care field, not to assume the roles of persons professionally trained in this area but in order to ask the right questions and assist community members in their decision-making.

9. *Death.* Quite a number of church groups have spent

time in recent years contemplating the subjects of death, dying, and suicide. Christians have distinctive views about the end of life in the body; to communicate these clearly, and to reaffirm our positions theologically, is both good and necessary. It is unfortunate that we have so often left persons wondering about and even obsessed by fear of the inevitable end of human life. Our Christian witness requires of us that we be specifically concerned to teach and learn about death and dying. It is not a topic only for the old and the infirm; children and youth encounter death, too, and they need to talk about it and form their views regarding it.

These nine areas I have listed here are elementary. They involve us all. They have to be faced in every community in a way that will be unique to it. No one in New York or St. Louis or Indianapolis or elsewhere can decide for the whole church what a given community believes and will strive to do about each one of these areas.

So there must be concerned teachers and learners in every community who bring to bear their best insights. In gatherings of persons (schools possibly, or other types of meetings), issues are faced and viewpoints are formed. And resolve is expressed to abide by community wisdom.

I am fully aware that such community effort is not now happening in most Christian churches. By that observation I mean merely that Christian educative effort is often missing. The community is not *at work,* through persons giving themselves unstintingly to a ministry of teaching, in order to make such an effort.

Teachers Wanted

I do not believe the effort is missing because people will not respond to it. It is missing because the people long for, hunger for, *teachers* who will take the lead and facilitate the process of crystallizing community insight and resolve. We suffer from a loss of leadership. Christian educators who insist on defining their work in generalized terms are forgetting such specific, life-oriented issues as the nine areas I have listed. The fuzziness of the general can surely give way to the clarity of specifics if we will work at it. To do so, we have to bring to bear the best of Biblical scholarship, and the best of our various theological and churchly traditions, including time-honored customs. The combining of the best out of our past with the wisdom we can muster from present studies will lead, with God's help, to an enriched community life. And it will happen because of teachers who say: "Come now, let's work on these matters that concern us so much. Let's find out what we believe as Christians and act upon it." This is community at work. It is education in the finest, most specific sense.

But more than that, it is a way of viewing Christian education as a part of the order of creation. We were made by God and set in this world with these specific, daily problems and issues to face: our sex roles; our home life; our roles as citizens; our health, clothing, and shelter; seedtime, harvest, and husbandry; finances; sickness and death.

Each of these matters involves the work of the Creator in giving us our bodies, our freedom, and our world to live in. Each demands of us that we bring into play our creative best as co-laborers with God. The care of the world is our responsibility, given to us by the Creator. And because of our Lord Jesus Christ, who has brought a new and joyful dimension to life, we care all the more about everything that affects the community. He is at work in this very body to "make all things new." That is the foundation of Christian education, and that is what makes it specific and (in the very best sense) *earthy.*

So it makes sense for kindergarten children, with their teachers, to be planting and tending gardens, visiting farms and dairies, factories and offices, hospitals and cemeteries.

It makes sense for children and adolescents to dig away

in Scripture and in books, to engage in energetic conversation, drama, role play, and dozens of other teaching/learning strategies devoted to life issues.

It makes sense for adult discussion groups, field trips, and special seminars to be scheduled and repeated again and again. Here is where people bring their best thoughts to bear upon matters in which they are all involved each day. It may seem for a time that they are "going around and around," or speaking only truisms. But the sensitive teacher, the incisive educator, will help them to cut through now and then, and participants will say, "Now I see something I hadn't understood before." The community will have been *at work* in a specific, educative task.

The reader may argue that I have committed the same blunder of generalization that I lamented in the first part of this chapter. Have I not brought under the Christian education umbrella virtually the whole of human life from birth to death? How can I speak of so *much* as "specific" rather than general? I respond:

Each local gathering of Christians, with their educators/teachers, has to select priorities and decide where to begin and which emphasis to adopt as the thrust, the direction, of that community's educative effort. It may be that a given parish will decide that its "mark," its critical emphasis, is going to be health care. Another may decide to work in the area of citizenship/leadership. Another may become the parish that works on financial decisions and their attendant value systems. I would not insist that every parish has to worry all the time about everything; it is too much to ask. One can be concerned about the totality of life without having to be educated in everything.

Think, for instance, of the colleges that have chosen to work hardest in certain areas while not diminishing the value of other fields of inquiry. Here is a college that is noted for its English department and journalism classes. Another is best known for its premedical courses. Still another is a leading institution for the study of music.

The point is that these colleges have achieved a community identity. They have worked out a direction, a thrust. It belongs to faculty, students, everyone connected with the institution. That is education—moving in a *direction* that is specific and defined.

The same can be true, I believe, of Christian education. Each parish or local body will ·determine its thrust, its focus. And leadership will work to make a "mark" in that direction. That is not to deny the necessity for an ecumenical view of the whole church in the whole world; it is simply to say that each part of the body has found its special task to work on. It could be quite exciting and give to Christian education a new sense of vitality and purpose.

8 / Combining Liturgy
with Educative Effort

Education is a specific effort to supply direction and thus to provide distinguishing characteristics for a community. Teaching occurs, and learning happens, within an educational framework that visualizes an outcome of some sort. It is this intentional aspect of a community's effort in teaching and learning that we name "education."

Christian education is no less specific. It visualizes an outcome—a people with distinguishing marks of their faith. Faith itself is a gift that is not produced by anything a teacher may do. But teaching and learning furnish understanding and refinement in the lives of the faithful. Conscious planning for specific directions and thrusts that Christian communities, and individuals within them, may take is the educative effort we name "Christian education." The educational task is to enable a people to work out their "style"—their special way of exhibiting what it means to be Christian in daily life.

One distinguishing mark of any particular church's life is the form of its Sunday worship. We can note great diversity in public worship of Christians. Having been engaged for many years in an ecumenical ministry of education, I have attended worship services in a wide variety of churches. Sometimes I have entertained whimsical thoughts about how it must seem to God to witness so many types of Christian worship. Perhaps it is pleasing to God to know that people have designed all these ways of praying, singing, and administering the Sacraments. Perhaps God tires of sameness and enjoys the array to the utmost. I hope it is not irreverent to imagine God listening in to a Mass and being pleased by the care with which it is done. Then a spirited Baptist revival session is heard in heaven with joy because of its zeal and sincerity. Next a Presbyterian service with a long and scholarly sermon delights the courts in heaven. That is followed by a Pentecostal meeting that offers ecstasy in place of form and logic, but it is accepted along with all the other offerings by the loving God to whom it is addressed.

No doubt I am imputing to God the sorts of feelings *I* have had through the years; I have derived spiritual benefit from worshiping in many kinds of settings, with persons representing a broad spectrum of theologies and customs. While I love my own tradition and do not intend to leave it, I am grateful for the contributions of others whose communities are also witnessing to our Lord.

We speak of churches as either liturgical or nonliturgical. The liturgical church follows an established form for public worship that is printed and used by the worshipers; more often than not, the Eucharist (Lord's Supper) is at the center of the liturgy. Celebrations of other hours of worship, and observance of special times of prayer, may not be eucharistic, but they all proceed from and point toward the act of Holy Communion.

For me, the most remarkable thing that has happened in my years of ministry was the Vatican II decision to allow the Roman Catholic Mass to be celebrated in the languages of the people. The simplicity of the service, seen now to be not only a priestly sacrifice but also an act of common worship involving the people in a most significant way, has been wonderfully inspiring to many observers in the Protestant traditions. Indeed, the liturgical revisions and renewal that have occurred in the Anglican (Episcopal) tradition, in the Presbyterian and Reformed family, in the United Methodist churches, and in the various Lutheran bodies, as well as in other denominations, have all reflected a much deeper understanding of our common roots in Western liturgical practice. The orders for the celebration of the Lord's Supper in these non-Roman Catholic churches are strikingly similar to the new Mass. This is not surprising, for the liturgical movement is clearly concerned to be faithful to long-held and cherished understandings of Scripture as well as ecclesiastical tradition.

The worship of Orthodox bodies and the Eastern Catholic churches follows ancient liturgical forms that stand quite apart from the Western traditions. But no Christian in attendance could fail to sense the centrality of the Scriptures, the bread and the wine, the acts of prayer, and the sermon for the hearing of the faithful.

It seems to me that the calendar of the Christian year is emerging in the consciousness of the free, nonliturgical churches as well. Some of the Southern Baptist churches are observing the Sundays of Advent in preparation for Christmas and finding it quite acceptable to their free, autonomous way of viewing worship and practice. More and more free churches speak of special Lenten observances, and the season of Pentecost is also better known and understood than in former years.

Using the Lectionary to Educate

Now we have available for our use in many churches a lectionary for the church year that is virtually uniform across Catholic-Protestant boundaries. In a three-year cycle, readings from Old Testament, Epistles, and Gospels have been selected for the seasons of the church year. They are sensitively arranged, and they make good sense to laypersons as well as to the clergy. I suspect that these lectionaries are now a part of the approved documents for worship in churches representing at least 75,000,000 Americans.[35]

Clergy have for the most part overlooked the enormous

potential of the lectionaries for focusing the attention of all people to the good news of God. Everyone who has analyzed the problems of communication in our modern culture has pointed to the necessity of choosing key themes and riveting the attention of the masses to their import; this is said to involve publicizing through multimedia approaches. It requires unity of effort between local and national "campaigns," and it means costly investment of time, energy, and money to bring such an effort into the public consciousness.

Well, here is the lectionary—already in the hands of millions of persons, already providing potentially a unifying theme week after week. Most of the hard work in selecting and publishing the Scriptural texts has already been done. It remains only for an imaginative clergy, working within their separate and honored traditions, to hold up this good news and let it speak full-voiced to the people!

But it doesn't happen. We are so protective of our right of individual choice that even the liturgical bodies can sometimes be cavalier about these chosen weekly readings. Priests, ministers, rectors, deans—they all decide to preach now and then "outside the lectionary," or to allow the reading to be subordinate to their own selected themes for sermonizing.

If I were a well-known evangelist, I would see in these lectionaries a welcome opportunity. Week after week I would preach from these readings, letting all my evangelistic appeals be related to the texts that are read in thousands of churches. People would see that my work as evangelist was directly related to the weekly worship experiences of millions of Christians throughout the world.

A few years ago a national evangelical effort was mounted with the slogan "I found it!" In newspapers, on radio and television, and through telephone contact, these zealous campaigners were trying to reach people with an evangelistic message. They spent millions of dollars for this flash-in-the-pan sort of activity. One can only wonder what might have happened if they had simply built their total effort around the Scripture readings used by millions of men and women in Christendom.

If the evangelists are insensitive to such opportunities for communication, Christian educators surely should not be. The lectionaries have enormous potential for teaching and learning if we would only seize the chance to utilize them effectively.

Here and there, a parish pastor will sense this opportunity to relate weekly worship to the programs of study among the people—both at church and in their homes. But it is a long way from being a widespread practice.

Church curricular resources, whether published by the denominations or by independent firms, seldom bear distinct relationship to the church year and the lectionary. Only at Christmas and Easter would one be likely to find genuine correspondence between the teaching guides and the liturgical year.

Let us consider the positive aspects of the idea of utilizing the lectionary in church education:

The readings are not long passages, for the most part. They have been chosen to highlight main themes in Scripture and in the Christian life. The context can be quickly determined through the use of a simple commentary. A few background paragraphs will usually assist the layperson to understand the context.

We can easily picture any parish, Catholic or Protestant, in which the families and individual members received a printed listing—in advance—of each week's readings. (The missals and other books that contain these readings are too complicated for most people; one may easily lose one's place and wonder where to turn next.)

It is best if a simple listing (or printing of the passage) is provided for each week. Then no one needs to wonder, Are we on the right Sunday's readings?

Some simple what-to-do guidance can be provided for households so that the coming week's readings are studied and pondered Monday through Saturday. And this can usually be done for every age level in a household, from preschoolers through adults.

Then, on the Sunday the readings are heard at public worship, the whole family listens with keenest interest. Children nudge their parents to indicate, "That's what we talked about at home!" And everyone waits with interest as the preacher uses these readings in weaving a meaningful sermon. The educative effect could be truly noteworthy, with all these elements working in concert: family reading and discussion; public worship and homiletic effort; back-home reflection on the day's preaching after church attendance.

Such a process could happen just as easily in a nonliturgical church as well. The only element that is absolutely essential is advance planning. Someone has to think through, for the local situation, just how to relate Scripture readings used in worship to the common life of the people —in advance, so that study is preparatory to worship, and worship follows reflection on the part of teachers/parents/learners.

Possibly one of the reasons this sort of educational strategy has yet to be employed is simply that we are unaccustomed to thinking about the task of interpreting Scripture for all age levels, and in a variety of ways.

Biblical material may be interpreted at these three levels:

1. The surface level of listening for facts (literal interpretation).
2. The level of the theological or churchly interpretation (looking for concepts and emphases that impel the church as a whole).
3. The somewhat transcendent level of searching for universal meanings related to human experience in every age.

Consider, as an example, Acts, ch. 3. Here is a story of a miracle performed by Peter and John. They heal a lame man, and this act attracts a crowd of amazed people. Peter uses the occasion to declare that it is by the power of Jesus Christ, the risen Lord, that the healing has occurred. He appeals to his listeners to hear God's special message: to repent of their sins and receive forgiveness. It is a good story that can be told to persons of all ages—children, youth, adults. Certainly the reader/listener can interpret at Level 1—it is a historical account of the apostolic period; it is something that happened involving three human beings, long ago. (The "deep structure" of Level 1 is simply "apostolic history.")

The church, the ecclesia, will see in the chapter an opportunity to interpret at Level 2. Peter and John are observing the fixed hour of prayer. Their work in the act of healing is the beginning of the church's ministry of healing; the apostles were in charge, and their leadership was blessed with special power from God. Christ's ministry is mediated through chosen leaders in the succession of the apostles. Preaching of repentance and forgiveness is linked with the resurrection experience, and Peter announces the work of Christ as the fulfillment of Hebrew prophecy; the descendants of Abraham are now the recipients of good news prepared for them from the beginning. The key words are prayer, healing, ministry, apostolic witness, prophecy's fulfillment, resurrection, repentance, and forgiveness. These are words of great importance to the continuing life of the church and to our theological understanding. (The "deep structure" of Level 2 is "Christian ministry.")

But it is certainly possible for us to find in this passage of Scripture a sort of transcendent, universal meaning (Level 3). In the healing of a lame man, the church affirms that restriction of movement (any form of "lameness" or inability to go where one wishes to go) is opposed to the will of God for human beings. We are created free and are meant to be able to walk on our own feet. Unjust political restrictions, racial segregation and discrimination, economic oppression and poverty—these are forms of lameness in our world. The liberating power of the Christian gospel, when brought to bear against all human lameness, is capable of setting people free and in a right, restored relationship with God and other persons.

The passage, thus universalized at a Level 3 interpretation, becomes a highly contemporary message. It addresses itself to us at whatever point of application is most apt at a particular place and moment. Are people "lame" within a stone's throw of our gathering place as Christians? If so, we are needed as instruments to heal their lameness and set them free as Peter and John did with the lame man. We may pray to be used of God in the act of lifting up our brothers and sisters who need to be freed from restrictions over which they are themselves powerless, perhaps from birth, as the man in the story. (The "deep structure" of Level 3 is "empowering freedom.")

The teacher/educator in the church will always be looking for these *levels* of interpretation in relation to passages of Scripture. In Year B, on the third Sunday of Easter, the Lectionary includes lines from Acts, ch. 3. The interpretation of these lines will be possible at all the levels I have described: (1) that of a "good story"; (2) that of a charter for the church's ministry; (3) that of a universal call to do battle against "lameness" in the world.

In the week preceding the reading of that passage, every person in a given church's parish could be reading and pondering: What does this say to me? When the preacher speaks from the pulpit, will it be with a special insight to complement, or add to, my own conclusions?

Parents can tell the story of the lame man to their children, then wait for the questions: How could Peter and John do that? Why don't such things happen to people we know? Discussions about the means of healing, in the hands of caring Christians, will be appropriate. Children can draw pictures, make tape recordings, or dramatize the story—with the help of family members.

Parents and adolescents can discuss the church's ministry and the special calling of certain men and women to serve human needs and to proclaim the Word in clear and certain terms. Training and development of ministers includes clinical pastoral education as well as theological and homiletical courses.

Family members can focus on the term "lameness." Does it always refer only to physical handicaps? What are some other kinds of restricted movement that we could term being "lame"? What are the causes of these other forms of human lameness? What are we asked to do about them?

These specific focuses of attention are enough to keep a typical family busy Monday through Saturday. Imagine how exciting it could be to come to church on Sunday after a week of contemplating the reading; it is the third Sunday after Easter, and the marvelous good news of the resurrection, celebrated only two weeks ago, is still fresh in everyone's mind. Now the minister or priest is speaking about what happened in the lives of the apostles as the church began to gather in those glad days. The sermon includes a call to ministry, and it offers possibly a conscience-pricking reminder of the kinds of lameness that are present right here in our community. We can be a part of the miracle-working of God if we do something to loose the bonds of restricted neighbors; as Easter people, we are no less responsible to declare the good news in word and deed than Peter and John.

Suppose that such a thrust of earnest study and contemplation of Acts, ch. 3, had occurred in community after community, throughout the nation, during that week! Would it not be a sparkling instance of the best sort of educative effort? Not that we would all conclude the same things about the passage or engage in platitudes about it. Far from it. We would see, each in our own direction-giving community, what these lines of Scripture meant for us, here and now. The fact that so many Christians would be laboring on the same passage at the same time would simply attest to our unity in the process of searching for meaning, a form of Christian unity that makes good sense from virtually any perspective. It is a *planned* unity, to be sure, but it requires no uniformity of liturgical practice beyond the simple act of using a selected passage of Scripture in a given week.

Growth Through Prayers

Another distinguishing mark of a Christian community will be the prayers of the clergy and of the people. It is a curious phenomenon that many of the free churches, turning aside from any established orders of liturgy and disdaining printed prayers, will exhibit a quite impersonal approach to public prayer. Petitions are general in many of the prayers, and the impression often left with the worshiper is that the prayers become another means of theological or evangelical exhortation. Sometimes the prayers sound surprisingly like small sermons cast in the form of pleas that God will help the people to understand what they should!

It might come as a real surprise to leaders of worship in these nonliturgical settings to discover that the prayers of their neighbors in liturgical, highly formal worship will often be quite personal and specific: thanksgiving for joys celebrated in the parish (births, marriages, graduations, new jobs), and petitions for God's succor for the sick, the bereaved, and the troubled. Names are mentioned, and the prayers are direct and heartfelt, shared by clergy and people. In many communities, the worshipers play a vital role in suggesting the content of the "prayers of the people."

In addition to simply asking people to say aloud what they wish to include in the day's prayers, some pastors have asked for written suggestions.

On a Sunday when I visited the old Second Presbyterian Church, in Richmond, Virginia, the pastor asked the people to write their special petitions on cards that were delivered to him and included in the service. The cards included prayers for world peace, for the President and the Congress, and this unforgettable line: "Please help my mother and daddy to let me have a gerbil I want so much."

At St. John's United Church of Christ, in Lansdale, Pennsylvania, a pedestal holds a large book, something like a guest register. As people enter the nave, they may write in the book, on that day's page, their special requests for prayer. The pastors receive the book at an appointed time in the service, and the prayer requests are solemnly read.

All such efforts in worship, even if they seem contrived, are meant to encourage prayer in relationship to active interest in others' welfare, and to bring daily piety into conjunction with real-life concerns and needs. The effect of common prayer in the life of the community is educative. Prayer has a direction-setting function.

Christian educators have neglected sadly the task that is uniquely theirs to assist children, youth, and adults to grasp the nature of prayer and to make it a regular part of their daily lives—just as essential to health as eating and sleeping. It is possible to teach people, by precept and example, how to engage in both private and corporate prayers to God. Drawing together in the exercises of piety, and especially in prayer, assists us in concentrating on our discipleship; thus our spiritual energies are concentrated rather than dissipated. This makes for an educative result.

Even Announcements Teach

Still another interesting facet of community gatherings of Christians is "announcement" time. The kinds of things that are announced are clear signals of what is important to the community, of the directions that have highest priority. Are they self-serving announcements, designed to shore up the institutional, programmatic life of the parish such as pleas for attendance at various committee meetings? Or do the announcements suggest opportunities for serving others, for meeting human need, for "rising to the occasion" of facing a crisis that has appeared?

When I was a parish pastor I was wrong about the matter of announcements. I assumed that if something appeared in the church's worship bulletin or in a letter to the people, that was enough. I thought it foolish to clutter up our public gatherings with announcements. But I am certain now that I missed a thoroughly educative opportunity. The personal announcement, stressed with the inflections of the human voice, is essential to the life of the community.

Sometimes it is the announcements that call forth the best in people and provide a sense of community that no amount of striving in other ways can achieve. I became aware of this in my visits to a score of theological seminaries in the last ten years.

Invariably, there is much talk on a seminary campus about the state of the "community." The students can usually find a lot that is wrong with community life, and they seek many avenues for attacking the problems. This is right and good; the criticism can be healthy. But what is frequently overlooked is that the true sense of community often appears in response to announcements rather than calculated efforts to "improve our community."

The seminary I know best is Louisville Presbyterian. Its campus is divided by a ravine. Most married students and their families live on one side of the ravine, and the single students live on the other side. The faculty live off campus. So there are three communities. But "announcement time" in chapel, and written notices on central campus bulletin boards, provide the necessary uniting element.

Students at Louisville were always saying to me that there was a lack of "community" on the campus. The problem was not nearly so severe as they perceived it, however. Just after commencement in the last year I was there, a graduating senior was seriously burned in a cooking accident. For weeks he underwent treatment, including skin grafts. He had been called to a parish in another state. Would you believe it? Faculty members took turns and traveled to that young man's future parish to serve on weekends! That's an expression of genuine community, and it manifested itself in response to the *announcement* of a member's need.

Another school of theology that has interested me very much is St. Paul's United Methodist Seminary in Kansas City. Every day, at lunchtime, everyone gathers in the large dining room for a common meal. "Everyone" includes faculty and their spouses, secretaries and other employees, students and their spouses and children. They all come together to eat, pray, and sing. Then there are two periods of announcements. Period I is announcements about campus concerns: meetings, lost-and-found, special needs of individuals. Period II is "concerns of the world": opportunities to give money, volunteer service, or vocal support to a variety of causes (missions, political groups, specific projects related to hunger, justice, and the like).

I am impressed by this determined effort to bring people together for announcements that supply direction to the life on that campus. Alumni of the school have told me how much they missed it when they left.

These campus-related examples have their counterparts in local parishes.

Every parish minister can attest to the way in which people will respond to emergencies within the community. It has something to do with the educative (direction-giving) effect of announcements, the way in which calls for service are laid before the people.

Similarly, the well-planned announcement time from week to week will produce an informed and participating people. Not everyone will respond, but a significant number will. Raising needs to the consciousness of people will sensitize their consciences to their servant roles, their common ministry in the world.

I wonder what would happen if Christian educators and pastors would spend some time together considering how to do really effective "announcing" in the community. The educative, direction-giving effect might be far-reaching. It appears that the process is necessarily linked with worship. The prayers and offerings of the people, and the gathering around the Lord's Table to celebrate Christ's gift of new life, call for active means of response. In hearing the announcements, and in echoing "Here am I! Send me," the worshipers commit themselves anew to co-laboring (collaborating) with the Lord in that continuing work of making "all things new"!

Understanding Worship

But let us turn to another, possibly more academic topic: enabling the people of God to take part in liturgy or worship with a greater sense of understanding, so that everything that is done, by clergy and people, is seen in a context of meaning.

It seems to me that people in gatherings for worship should be able to answer questions like the following:

What is the story of the Apostles' Creed? Why is it used week after week?

Why is the Trinitarian formula used in every baptism?

Why was the Gloria Patri introduced into worship? When should it be sung?

These are only a few of many questions that should occur to inquisitive people. The questions have answers. The answers will differ according to persons' traditions, possibly, but they are important nonetheless.

Other questions that arise out of tradition would have to do with the garb worn by clergy. Why, for instance, does a Presbyterian clergyman insist on an academic gown such as the kind worn in Geneva, Switzerland, in the time of John Calvin? What significant changes have been made in the robing of Catholic clergy in recent years? Why? Bishop Stephen Neill, Anglican, once said that all clothing is ultimately ridiculous, but still there are reasons why people dress as they do. They are related to deep-seated conviction, or at least they once were. Would it not be appropriate for the people in general to know?

Then there are the symbols used in furnishings, tapestries, linens, and hangings, in our churches. Surprisingly few laypersons are aware of their meanings and origins. Such knowledge is not a life-or-death matter, of course. Certainly it has nothing to do with the salvation of humankind. Still, Christians do have symbols and things of aesthetic value to be treasured. It is right that people should have an opportunity to appreciate them as a result of being informed.

Some years ago I was invited to teach a course on Christian symbolism at the Cook Christian Training School, Tempe, Arizona. It was a wonderful class. Among the students was a middle-aged woman who was a member of the Sioux tribe in the Dakotas. She was an Episcopalian and a longtime member of the altar guild in her church. One day, as we were discussing the symbols related to the Eucharist, I noticed tears streaming down her cheeks. I was solicitous to find out what I had inadvertently said or done to disturb her. She explained: "All these years I have looked at these symbols in my church and have seen them embroidered on the linens I washed and cared for. I never knew before what they meant, and I am crying because it means so much to me to find out."

Christians have little consensus on the value of symbols. Some believe they are lifeless and have little more value than a "dead language." Others see in them the possibility for enhancing meaning and communication.

Over twenty-five years ago, I was taking a visiting church executive through the little church where I was pastor in Missouri. He frowned disapprovingly when I showed him the new antependia the women of the church had just made, to conform to the established colors of the liturgical year. "This sort of thing gets in the way of evangelism and leads to low vitality in parish life," he pronounced. I felt as if I had just flunked out.

Are such matters considered adequately these days by church educators? Something tells me that the time is right for renewed interest in symbolism. It's a kind of right-brain interest that we have neglected. Symbols can speak of truths hard to express in analytical language. Still, they cannot be used with full appreciation unless we do some educative, community-wide explaining and appreciating.

One of the most interesting efforts in this direction that I have ever seen is in the Church of the Blessed Sacrament, Scottsdale, Arizona. A colleague of mine is the former minister of education there, and he shared it with me.

As children in that parish approach the time of their "first Holy Communion," they are given individual squares of white cloth. Each child is permitted to decorate that square in any appropriate way to express something of the meaning of this significant event. The children take the squares home and add symbols and decorations that speak of their personal lives and the church. Then the squares are collected and sewn together to form an altar hanging. As the new communicants and their parents come into the church on that important Sunday morning, they see their work—all sewn together symbolically to speak of their unity at the Lord's Supper. What's more, the hangings from all the previous years are displayed around the walls of the nave. It's exciting and meaningful to every participant, and it will become more so as the tradition is preserved.

This is symbolism in a new key. It has to do with both cognition and affect.

Perhaps the essence of relating education to worship/

liturgy is summed up in the words "participation" and "explanation." I am indebted to Father Alexander Schmemann for bringing this to my attention in a fresh way.[36] In his Orthodox tradition, the liturgy in its true sense of "the work of the people" is all-important and central. The people of God need to participate in it fully and in deepest reverence. But that participation is enhanced and given its quality of vitality when a continuous process of explanation is present in the people's lives— hence, the need for educative effort, for teaching (showing and patiently pointing to meaning and the essential concepts).

Historically, monastic or cloistered life was an accommodation to the hard reality that all people could not spend time in meditation, reading, praying. The lives of the masses were taken up in the difficult struggles of daily work, and literacy for all was not a primary concern. Religious communities preserved the Scriptures and functioned in the people's behalf.

Later centuries brought remarkable breakthroughs for the common people. The Scriptures became available, thanks to printing. The educational standards were raised —ever so slowly (much more slowly for women than for men), but raised they were. The possibility of much wider involvement in informed, meaningful liturgy became available to people.

Bursts of evangelical fervor sometimes resulted in sheer iconoclasm. Ancient symbols and forms were often discarded in the zeal to reach people's hearts with the gospel message. The ever-present tensions of the charismatic vs. the more formal styles of worship produced excesses in all directions. These are apparent in both Protestantism and Catholicism.

So today one is confronted with a confused state, liturgically speaking. One wonders how to make sense of it. One Sunday not too long ago I listened to a Presbyterian choir singing marvelous anthems in Latin, straight out of the

Middle Ages. On that same weekend I attended a Catholic Mass where the music was provided by guitar and the modern lyrics were vacuously sentimental and ordinary. What a strange turning of the tables!

Where does one find authenticity in worship—direction-giving, educative effort linked with spiritual power and fervor?

Possibly one has to go back to the monastic setting again. If one visits a seminary of the Benedictines, for example (the kind of Roman Catholic setting I know best), here will be found these elements in abundance: careful use of Scripture both in the readings and in the homilies; music of great beauty; simple but powerful works of art; great warmth of spirit in the celebration of the Eucharist. One comes away, or at least I do, saying: "What a gift to the world, in our Lord's name! If only the people in the parishes could be here to take part." I wonder, too, whether there will ever be a time when men and women will serve in such a setting, standing on equal ground. It seems to my Protestant soul that someday they must!

In contrast to such worship, the Protestant seminaries have a long way to go. Chapel services are impoverished in seminaries of the main-line Protestant denominations. Liturgies are ill-prepared and highly individualistic. The kind of vitality in common prayer and singing that we witnessed in the years following World War II and continuing through the early 1950's has all but disappeared. Why has this happened? Oddly, the worship in individual parishes is far more vital and intelligently offered than in the seminaries of the Protestant churches.

What a rich opportunity Christian educators/teachers have before them! They know how to teach, how to activate. They know a lot about how people learn. So why not move into the breach and do something significant about common worship?

This is not the Middle Ages. People do not have to work all the time. Their health is good. They live longer. They can read and reflect, for they have time that could be given to these activities.

There is no good reason why powerful worship cannot be offered, week after week, to Almighty God. People have to be taught how to take part; a lot of good explaining needs to be done, followed by practice and participation. Worthy worship can be happening everywhere, not just in special religious communities. Why not?

Imagine an army of concerned Catholic, Anglican, Orthodox, Reformed, Methodist, Baptist, and Pentecostal (just to mention a few) clergy and lay leaders who would march upon the churches and declare: Let's offer our best to Jesus Christ in our worship: the best in readings of Scripture, the best in homilies and sermons, the best in music, the best in announcements. And let's involve all the people in renewal so that their worship takes on an indispensable, life-giving role in their rhythms of life.

I see that as a primary educational function, specific, arising out of community and, in turn, giving direction and life to the community.

I am not pleading here for uniformity. No one needs to relinquish his or her heritage in order to take on someone else's. My thesis is that *each* heritage can revitalize worship through common, educative effort. It is a matter of locating where the essential knowledge and vitality now exist (and I gave a Benedictine seminary as just one prime example), and taking steps to magnify that sort of worship so that it appears in the common life of people.

Someone may say: "But the times are just not conducive to such an effort. You can't find enough concerned people to make it happen."

To this objection I can only point to such phenomena as these in our culture:

Fraternities and sororities have been experiencing a revival. Their officers and members spend many hours practicing and conducting their rituals in a really vital way. Why would such a thing happen when only a few years ago it was predicted that fraternal organizations were on their way out of campus and community life? It suggests to me that people hunger for the opportunity to take part in meaningful ritual. What if a parish's educational leaders would spend as much time helping people to prepare for weekly worship as these fraternal groups often spend in the preparation for a special ceremony? There is explosive potential here.

Or consider the growth and development of community symphony orchestras in the last decade. Enter one of the concerts, and you will be handed a handsome booklet of program notes. Often a local writer has prepared highly instructive essays on all the pieces that will be played in that particular concert. People read these notes avidly as they await the entrance of the conductor and the first chords of the performance.

What would happen if the same sort of care were exercised in providing worshipers with "program notes" to offer the history and descriptive material about parts of the worship for a given week? It could happen, but only if Christian educators give partial or full assent to this proposition:

Worship and education belong together in our thinking. Forms of worship or liturgy are distinguishing marks among Christians. They give direction to the lives of Christ's people; they are a source of renewal. And educative effort is essential to the process.

9 / Reaching Into the World

No book about Christian education would be complete without some effort to relate the content to the issues of the larger world. We learn, we teach, and we gather in community, but not just to indulge our own internal needs. We care about what happens in the world, in the body politic, in the socioeconomic realm, for ours is a ministry of *healing* in Christ's name.

The awareness of what is happening in every part of the globe has added new burdens of responsibility for sensitive Christians. When upheaval in Asia, Africa, the Middle East, or elsewhere produces death, suffering, and injustice, the people of the churches cannot hide from it or disregard it. More than a subject for prayer, each instance of human suffering or oppression is a cause for action.

Concern for all peoples, in whatever circumstance, arises out of the Christian conviction that God's created world is meant to be the scene of redemption, or renewal and hope for new life. It is not, therefore, plausible that God's people will be indifferent to suffering, callous to injustice, or lethargic in the face of crisis.

While Christian bodies differ greatly regarding the appropriate method for assuming this sensitive, larger view of the world, they are united in affirming that Christians care and are called upon to act. Christians are responsible for healing.

My service as an ordained minister began just before the

1954 Supreme Court decision regarding the desegregation of public schools. I was a young pastor in a small Missouri town. We subscribed to the Sunday *New York Times,* thanks to a generous but conservative banker in our church. There I was able to read in detail the background articles on the court's historic decision, and to follow the news of reactions throughout the nation.

I wondered what would happen in our town's schools in the fall of 1954. A few people suggested there would be friction, possibly some real unpleasantness. We watched intently. But good sense prevailed, and integration proceeded with all deliberate speed. Black students were involved in every kind of school activity, so far as I could tell.[37] To the surprise of some adults in the community, the high school student body elected a black student as president. Some of the young people in our church said this special gesture happened to indicate that the white students were sorry for discrimination in the past, which had led to separate schools and virtually no interracial contact.

The next year I went to a national board of Christian education staff in Philadelphia as an editor of curricular materials. There, we were all caught up in publishing materials that would be helpful to youth in examining their feelings about race. It was an exhilarating time for the church. We were late in dealing forcefully with racism, but despite our tardiness we all did our part. In print, in public speech, and in political action we affirmed that God had made of "one blood" all the peoples of the world. The winds of social change were blowing strong and pure, and Christians were in the forefront of the civil rights movement of the 1950's and 1960's.

We still have far to go in combating racism. But sometimes I marvel at the distance we have traveled in my lifetime. Consider this example: In 1947, I had gone to a national convention of my college fraternity, held in the Deep South. For the first time in my life I saw separate facilities for colored people. I witnessed so many examples of segregation and its dehumanizing effects that the convention had scarcely any importance for me; it was the racial scene that made the strong impression. Part of my observations were made in Richmond, Virginia, where I spent several days during that trip.

In 1976, during the January term at Presbyterian School of Christian Education, in Richmond, I taught a course in the learning laboratory.[38] In the weeks of that course, we offered special modules of training for volunteer teachers in the churches in Richmond. The blocks were taught by my students, and quite a number of the participants from the city were black teachers. I sat observing the whole process, and I remembered 1947. I felt prompted to speak privately with one of the teachers engaged in a learning project near where I was sitting. She was a professor of education at a state institution. I said: "I have been sitting here remembering a trip to Richmond nearly thirty years ago. Things are so much better now, and I am so grateful." She grasped my hand, tears in her eyes, and she said, "Thank you, thank you, for remembering!"

When the visitors were gone, and just the students and I remained in the laboratory, I shared what had happened. To my dismay, the students (all in their twenties) looked at me in puzzlement. What was I talking about? they wondered. They didn't have any idea how the Richmond they knew differed from the Richmond of 1947! For a moment I was subject to quite a mixture of feelings:

I felt old and tired for having lived through so much, so quickly. I felt a sense of elation and joy that some progress had occurred in striking down old racial barriers that had been such a burden. And mingled with my downright regret that the students didn't appreciate what I had lived through was the sudden realization that these young people would be spared at least that chapter of American history. They could take up the cudgels at a different level altogether. And I was feeling grateful to God, who does indeed work in human affairs.

Using the Institution

The days of the civil rights movement overlapped with the period when so many critics lashed out at the church's ineffectiveness as an "institution." It was fashionable in some quarters to distinguish between the lethargic institutional church and the transcendent concept of the church as a faithful remnant of prophets set in a hostile world.

I was always uneasy about these severe condemnations of the word "institution." Civilization requires institutions, and I believe it is nothing short of anarchism to rail against them. Our hope for righteousness and justice in society does not lie in abolishing or crippling the government, the schools, the churches, and other establishments. Rather, it lies in maintaining a spirit of healthy, constructive *criticism,* aided by the concept of checks and balances in our democratic system. Management and labor, government and the constituency, marketing and consumers, schools and student bodies, and churches and civil communities—all these groups are part of a finely tuned instrument in the American experiment. We have our noisy and cacophonous times of confrontation, to be sure. Sometimes it appears that we are about to lose the vision and succumb to civil strife. We came so close to that in the period of the Vietnam war. But so far, the system is still working. The rule of law takes into account the rights of individuals and minorities; it is far from perfect in achieving the ideal of "justice for all," and we are always critical in the sense of wishing for things to be better than they are. But nowhere in the world is there a keener sensitivity to the ills of society than there is in America. Some of us are at times even more critical of ourselves than the situations warrant.

The sensitivity, the intelligent criticism, the pressing for effective social action, have their roots and are preserved in the churches and synagogues. These "institutions" are sustained from year to year by clergy, rabbinate, and laity. The Torah and the Gospel are proclaimed and bear fruit in our confessions and in our quickened consciences.

The Christian churches are the freest institutions of all. They adapt more easily to change, and they are able to marshal resources for action more quickly than any other bodies in our society.

Possibly a small episode will illustrate what I have just said about our freedom in the churches. As an editor of curricular resources in the 1950's, I was concerned about relating what we did in our published church materials to the textbooks used in public schools. It seemed to me that churches needed to be more attuned to the reading material provided in the schools so that the church school curricula would at least be commensurate (especially in typographical format, readability levels, and the like). So I set out to interview textbook editors in New York and Chicago.

The secular editors were cordial and more than generous in sharing their time and insights. They seemed as eager to find out what church curriculum editors were doing as I was to learn about their work.

I had taken with me sample magazines from the Christian Faith and Life curriculum, a program for church and home that featured magazines for parents and teachers of every age level. These magazines were nicely printed and typographically outstanding. They included many photographs in black and white.

As editors, we were making a conscious effort to include racial minorities in all these photographs, including the cover photos.

At a luncheon with a group of high school textbook editors, I passed the magazines around the table. They looked at one another in what I perceived to be a sort of agitated silence. Then one of the men said quietly: "We aren't yet free to use pictures like these in our textbooks. It would still be economically troublesome for our company, our salesmen in the South have warned us."

That comment broke the ice, and the group shared with me their anxieties about the whole matter. They were sensitive people caught in a dilemma. But their company had not found the courage to do what the church had done easily!

In that moment I felt extraordinarily grateful that the church was at least unfettered in this one simple respect; we weren't worrying about the consequences of affirming desegregation in our publications. We were free to bear witness, and we could marshal our resources quickly in efforts to heal the wounds of prejudice. Through the years as I have worked with consultants in the field of public education, I have been impressed again and again with the freedoms I enjoy in the church (as "institution," mind you).

The laboratory experiences I have designed and disseminated for the education of teachers have been admired by professors of education in universities. Their praise has been embarrassingly generous. And there is always the lament, "We aren't free yet to try these kinds of approaches in our university setting." It is really true that the nature of the church enables it to change and to act more quickly than other institutions.

I once asked Dr. Sara Little, then teaching at the Presbyterian School in Richmond, how it was that this small institution could remain strong in a time when so many other structures for Christian education were crumbling all around. She replied that the school had been deliberately changing its course offerings from year to year; it was responding constantly to needs expressed by a constituency. In short, this Christian institution could *change*. What was there to stop its efforts to innovate? Nothing, so long as its leadership was sensitive to an institutional image based on creative response to human need.

The institutional *health* of all Christian communities, and the accompanying ability to both initiate and respond to change, is due in no small measure to the Catholic-Protestant dialogue of recent years. The sweeping changes of Vatican II are seen by Protestant leaders to be the continuation of a process begun in the sixteenth century. The new catechesis in the American churches has produced a remarkable spirit of cooperation and sense of mutuality among Catholic and Protestant leaders who affirm their unity in "one Lord, one baptism." Stress upon the doctrine of the Holy Spirit gives a mighty thrust toward spiritual unity.

Nowhere has the sensed unity been made more apparent than in the civil rights movement and other social action programs that brought Catholic and Protestant shoulder to shoulder in common purpose. One must also take note of the tension we experience now on the issues of birth control and the ordination of women. Yet I would not rule out the possibility that someday we will be able to look back and say that the checks and balances in the process of debate, struggle, and confrontation eventuated in a healthy new approach to these issues as well.[39]

All these reflections on social awareness and social change in our time lead to the questions: What are the chief agents of change? What causes social action to take place?

Teachers and Prophets

I have to keep coming back to the classic answer: the agents of change are the teachers and the prophets. Both teachers and prophets help in the forming of community with its direction-giving, educative function in society. False teachers and false prophets also engage in formation of community, but their works condemn them. I dwell instead upon the teachers and prophets of Christ who strive within their established traditions to be faithful to God's Word.

I have used the civil rights movement as the prime

example of social awareness, action, and change. I chose this paradigm because we have more perspective upon it and can observe a greater consensus regarding it than we can on some of the other issues of recent years, such as the antiwar movement. But the principles that follow are applicable to all issues of social change:

1. *Teachers* work slowly, patiently, and thoroughly to activate sensitivity of conscience among all whom they touch. Their hope is that each student will create a role of obedience to Jesus Christ who is at work to make "all things new."

2. *Prophets* are the preachers who proclaim that the "time has come" to act on the good news, to demonstrate openly for justice and righteousness, to exhibit powerfully and radically that the "new creation" will not wait.

We need both teachers and prophets. There is a sense in which they check and balance one another within the church.

Sometimes in the 1960's I felt personally guilty because I was doing so little about civil rights in comparison with others I knew who were engaging in the marches, the sit-ins, the protests. But as I look back upon it, I believe sincerely that I was simply not given the gift of prophecy. Instead, I was a *teacher.* I cannot even estimate how many articles and lessons I wrote, how many classes I taught, that were devoted to civil rights. I am still doing it, still striking any blow I can against racism, still praying that I will be sensitive to the vestiges of it that have not been purged from my own soul. So far as I can tell, my gift is that of a teacher—and I should not feel guilty because God has given me only one gift instead of two.

Teachers must be grateful for prophets who do what teachers cannot. And prophets should be grateful for teachers who are so essential to the fullness of the church.

I think back to the influence of *teachers* in my own life as I coped with the racial issue. Born into a family with an essentially Confederate history, my youth was lived in an unchallenged setting of "separation." We had black servants in our home and on our farm. My father especially would have been incredulous at any attempt to "mingle," for it was simply socially unacceptable.

Two Presbyterian ministers pried my eyes open and taught me. They were not harsh or strident in what they said to me, but they raised questions. They activated thought I had never entertained before. I began to create painfully a new view of race relations, quite at odds with my childhood view. I learned.

There were other influences: the excellent radio programs produced by the NAACP, which provided so much background about the whole issue that I would not have been able to hear elsewhere; the conversations with college classmates and professors; the daily contacts in theological seminary with students who were black.

Years of teaching and learning made it possible for me to appreciate and respond to the prophets—to Martin Luther King, Jr., and his predecessors, to Andrew Young and others I came to know. As a teacher I could empathize totally with thousands of persons who had *not* been exposed to patient teaching in the field of race relations; they had a very difficult time of it when the prophets began to speak out and to arouse people to definitive action. Some of them reacted violently, and it was an ugly thing to see. But so it happens in every period of radical social change: teachers have been at work all along, paving the way to a degree. And the prophets play their distinctive role, pressing for action and voicing the cry for justice *now*.

Teachers have to see their role as patient cultivators of community. They supply direction; they have the essential educative motive. Thousands of pastors in both black and white churches in the South did just that—quiet, careful teaching of people. Roman Catholic bishops exerted their teaching role with firmness.

But then so do the prophets produce a sense of community, also supplying direction and serving an educative intent. The organized action groups, the boycotts, the protest marches—these are the tools the prophets used in forming their supportive communities across denominational lines, even across the differences of secularists and theologians.

Teaching is subject to forms of excess. It can be excessively patient and slow to urge decisive action. It can often obscure the facts with circumlocution.

Prophetic ministry is also subject to excesses. It can oversimplify, succumb to brute power, and produce painful alienation.

So teacher and prophet need each other. Each helps to check the other's excesses. Each functions as a gift of God to the church and the world. Neither can say that I have no need of the other, no more than eyes, ears, or feet can deny their need of other parts of the body. Paul made that so clear.

It seems quite clear to me that an understanding of the valid ministries of both teacher and prophet might have spared the churches some of the painful schisms endured in recent years over the issue of corporate vs. individual responsibility for social change.

When churches have produced the sort of consensus that led to corporate resolutions and group action, other groups have sometimes objected. The call to Christian action, they say, is a call to individuals, not to larger bodies. They speak of the work of evangelized Christians as faithful witnesses for social change in their daily lives, but they recoil from giving a blessing to a churchwide, corporate form of witnessing.

This overlooks important lessons of the past. It was corporate action that helped to establish American democracy in the first place; the churches were not timid about taking a stand during the Revolution. And in this century, the history of the world would have differed in a thousand respects if the churches of Germany *had* acted against

Hitler with the power they might conceivably have brought to bear.

The issue of corporate vs. individual action is not central. Much more to the point is the need to recognize the classic roles of teachers and prophets. Both conservatives and liberals in the churches should address themselves to supporting these mutually constructive ministries in the body of Christ, and to clarifying issues constructively rather than through name-calling, polarization, and schismatic accusation.

For my own part, I brood over the need for better teaching—teaching that draws upon the faithful interpretation of our heritage and ferrets out all that is needed for giving the community of Jesus Christ a clear sense of direction. Such teaching is needed if we are to sense something "educative" about our work in the world and are to relate meaningfully to the real issues of society and nation.

Key Words for Better Teaching

I have chosen seven key words that seem to me to describe the "better teaching" we need: observation, facts, debate, words, balance, priority, persistence.

1. *OBSERVATION.* Jesus asked his disciples to "discern this time" with the same skill they brought to predicting the weather through observation (Luke 12:56). Careful and discerning observation is a hallmark of effective teaching and learning (discipleship).

When preschool teachers take boys and girls to a fire station to see the equipment and to meet the fire fighters, they are taking early steps to help children sharpen their powers of observation. The process is never-ending. Children, youth, and adults need to scrutinize carefully how resources are managed, how decisions are made, and how every facet of life contributes to the whole—for good or ill.

That is why the communications media are so vital in a free society. They expose to the light what is going on in the world, and they facilitate constructive debate for the fostering of intelligent decision-making. The printing press enabled the church, historically, to make enormous strides in the application of the gospel to life. It was not printing for its own sake that did this; it was the use of the printed word to increase our ability to *observe*. And today the projected media (photographs, motion pictures, and television) bring an altogether new dimension. Cameras help us to observe intelligently, but they also distort observation because they see only partially; the picture that is worth "a thousand words" will not stand alone as a means of observation. The learner and the teacher must investigate the context with more than camera in hand.

Observation implies being *present* in order to *find out*. We were awakened in 1979, for instance, to a need to be more closely observant of the nuclear power industry. It was a healthy thing for responsible decision makers to have their work open to fresh, thorough scrutiny. And Christians could not opt for a stance against nuclear power development without full recognition that for many years it had been considered a good thing to support "peaceful uses of atomic energy"! What had been lacking between the time of advocacy of nuclear power, and the new awareness of the peril of nuclear accident, was vigilance in observation on the part of the rank and file as well as experts in the field.

Christian teachers encourage observation and data-gathering, whether in the academic chores of Bible study and theological reflection or in the consideration of contemporary issues. There can be no end to the need for carefully planned field trips and for dogged, individual effort to observe what is really happening all around us. We have the tools for observing; we need only the commitment to a process of investigation.

2. *FACTS.* Observations lead to conclusions. Teachers must be wary lest the conclusions are insupportable by facts. It is a truism that we are subject to propagandizing

effort on a scale never before imagined or possible. The same media that serve us so well in observing are potentially the means of propaganda as well.

In recent years I have spent more time with men and women close to the commercial world. Sometimes I listen in painful disappointment to what seem to me to be their blind spots—their insensitivity to some of the human needs I have observed and they have not. But more often, I am encouraged by how *well* they have informed themselves. They do not fit the stereotypes when considered individually. Each person has a special soft spot—a conscience sensitized. I could recount a hundred stories of effective social change for which these business leaders have been taking a quiet but firm stand for many years. No wonder they bridle against the charge that they have been callous on all counts, for their critics have not bothered to find out what is really going on.

It is the *facts* that have to be weighed. Teachers bear a great responsibility to get all, not part, of the facts. With the exposition of facts to scrutiny it should come as no shock to conservatives, for example, to discover that the "church bureaucracy" has been, after all, doing a fairly good job of administering their benevolence monies! No more than it should come as a shock to liberals that some members of the military-industrial complex, for example, are not guilty of all charges!

The times call for reasoned conclusions that sift out fact from propaganda and produce a climate of truth-seeking that clears the way for responsible Christian community. Such a climate is truly direction-giving (educative).

3. *DEBATE.* Reasonable people differ in the conclusions reached on the basis of the same facts. This happens because of deep-seated and recurring theological and philosophical positions.

In every generation, the same issues have to be reconsidered and debated. It always comes as a surprise to teenagers to discover, for instance, that their concerns about personal autonomy and responsible freedom are not alien issues to their parents. We have been this way before. Although each new generation faces elements of social interaction that are unique, the underlying philosophical issues do not change that much.

The church is the best possible debating society. It is committed to the "truth that sets [people] free," and it can never be content to declare its gospel without a willingness to let it be tested in the crucible of debate. Paul, the apostle, set that tone of intellectual honesty, and he was supported in it by the other apostles, from the Council at Jerusalem (A.D. 49) onward. The lamp of freedom has sometimes burned low in Christian history, and we are not proud of that; but it has never really gone out. The ministry of teaching, properly exercised, deliberately encourages open and honest debate within the church as well as between the church and its antagonists.

4. *WORDS.* It is axiomatic that a time of rapid social change produces so much hastiness of expression that there is little time for reflection, clarifying, and defining.

I believe that is where we are today. We seem somewhat loathe to focus clearly on the task of definition. So much of what is written is reflective of careless tendencies to use words and catchphrases without explaining what they mean. I have noticed, for instance, how the word "catechesis," prized by the Roman Catholic educationists and used in official documents of the church, seems to be elusive of definition. Why should it not be more clearly defined for the laypersons who wonder just what it means?

But that is a fairly esoteric example. Consider more earthy ones, such as power, justice, and peace. What do these words mean, historically? And how do Christians uniquely bring their creative minds into conjunction with them?[40]

I have spent years focusing on the words "teacher" and "teaching," only to find the clergy especially to be impatient and eager to leave all such definition to others. As a steady listener to sermons and homilies, I have noted over and over how semantically careless preachers can be, largely because of the burden of trying to say much in the short time available. Sometimes I think of what a liberating thing it might be if a sermon focused on a single word now and then, exposing the preacher's honest struggle in trying to make sense of it.

A few years ago, a friend and I visited Dr. Norton Beach, then dean of education at the University of North Carolina. We found in him a sympathetic listener as we sought his opinion about curriculum-building. We had asked if he thought we had a good case for a research project to identify some of the "key concepts" that should be arranged in sequence for a church's study. He indicated that he believed an entire senior high school curriculum could probably be constructed around a dozen key words.

Dr. Beach's conclusion had been based on a personal experience in which he had spent most of a summer in New York, studying the concept of "trust." Think of how that single word has generative power beyond measure in our society—all the way from parent-child relations to giant trust companies. And for Christians, it is virtually synonymous with the word "faith."

Teachers have a sacred obligation to deal with words with a sense of care bordering on reverence. Students who learn to love words have in their hands something indispensable to creating, making, building. The community of God's people feeds upon the richness of its language— spoken, sung, and *felt*. Living language supplies thrust and direction.

5. *BALANCE.* The diets of schools, educationists, and curricula are always in danger of imbalance, just as our natural diets may be long on carbohydrates and short on proteins. Literally hundreds of children have said to me, in one way or another, that they get bored in church school because "it's always the same thing."

When pressed to explain why it's the "same," they respond: The teachers "talk all the time" about Jesus, Moses, and love. So what else is there?

We have not asked ourselves with frequency, What is it that we are doing each time we are with our students that is *not* the same as last week or yesterday? Children are perceptive on this score—they know whether there is something different or whether they are simply being conned into reexamining something that is the same.

The richness of our Christian heritage would make it impossible for us to deal with all the possible avenues of exploration in a lifetime of Sundays. That's really true. So it is a real indictment against us that we have sometimes built flimsy study units that feature repetition ad nauseam. We build Nehemiah's wall a dozen times; once may be enough, at least until we discover something new about the story. We present even our Lord Jesus in a most unfair light if we fail to look for the unfathomable depths to his person. The radical ethical demands of the Christian faith depend on an understanding that is complex and multi-faceted rather than simple and limited in dimensions.

Of course, teachers have to "repeat" (as does curriculum). But there must be a search for balance—a concentrated effort to add depth where superficiality is the peril.

6. *PRIORITY.* I have not forgotten that this chapter is related primarily to social outreach of the Christian community.

Teachers, like all others, must recognize acute limitations of time, energy, and ability in relation to themselves especially. It is not possible to do a good job of teaching everything one would like, even about a single concept.

Dr. Harry Emerson Fosdick is reputed to have said that every clergyperson can take on only one big "battle" in a lifetime. His chosen battle happened to be the bitter fundamentalist/modernist controversy. But for others since Dr. Fosdick, the principle seems to hold fairly well. It is just not possible to take on every cause, every issue, with the same vigor. One has to be modest enough to allow others to have their day of battle. One can be supportive and helpful without being always on the battlefront.

Even in our weekly or daily contacts with students in classes, teachers have to set priorities. We cannot avoid the necessity of asking, What is most important to teach/learn right *now?* This is different from "balance." Here I am thinking of the necessity of weighing a variety of teaching/learning tasks and choosing on the basis of what is most urgent or needful in this very place, this unique community.

One of the vexing problems of using prepared curriculum resources, however good they may be, is that the materials themselves often seem to set our priorities. We have to resist that and be willing to think of what is best for our students in our own situations. That requires a great deal of prayer and consultation, especially with other teachers and planners on the church school staff. We are tempted to teach what satisfies "our" needs, or what we may feel more "comfortable" about teaching.

The context of societal issues (politics, economics, and international relations, and moral or ethical dilemmas) will, in the sensitive Christian community, have a lot to do with how priorities are set for the educative effort. One must listen for the words of the prophets as well as our own counsel as we set about choosing.

7. *PERSISTENCE.* I can name at least twenty young friends, men and women, who went eagerly from their theological studies into educational ministries. Their stories differ a great deal in detail, but one thing they have in common: they all quit.

There seems to be a sense of loneliness and frustration in the field of Christian education that is unbearable for a lot of gifted people. That is painful to observe and to write about.

Some professional organizations in the churches have sought to do battle with this issue by an emphasis upon more rights, better pay, improved status for the recognized office of a Christian educator/teacher. Perhaps that is needed, but I am not sure it is the most appropriate answer.

Teaching is, by its very nature, not a profession that yields a lot of tangible returns—and especially not in the first decade or so. Senior clergy can speak somewhat expansively about the buildings they have caused to be erected, the church attendance they have caused to grow, the evangelizing they have done that increased membership, and so on. Why should we be overcritical of them for doing so? They have the right to speak of personal achievements of this sort.

But the teacher who has simply tried to be faithful in activating thought and whose whole life is given to helping students to create for themselves frequently is never able to know whether anything at all has resulted from the work. Students are rarely inclined to tell their teachers what they have been learning (creating inwardly). Indeed, the students may not even realize that it was a teacher who got something going for them; that may be a fact lying dormant and unrecognizable for years to come.

Small wonder, then, that we "lose heart" and feel lonely in a ministry of teaching. Did our Lord feel less lonely, less deserted?

Persistence, sticking to the task, rising again and again to the demand of discipleship—this is what teachers have to do. And especially if they are to play that necessary healing role in helping the church of Christ to reach out meaningfully, actively, into a world of human need.

These seven key words have been especially helpful to me in times of stress and discouragement. Perhaps they are the same words that sustain a prophet issuing a clarion call to action. In any case, they will not allow us to take our ease. We work and face ahead in Christian community—Orthodox, Catholic, and Protestant, conservative and liberal, individuals and covenanting groups—for the "night is coming" when our "work is done." The fever of life will be over, and in the hush we shall listen *together* (prophets, teachers, evangelists, everyone). Will we hear our Lord's, "Well done . . ."?

A Conclusion

Earnest discussions about the state of the churches' teaching ministry are not happening on any wide scale. Relatively few books are being written in the field of Christian education. Not many names in church education are well known, and the ones we might recognize are hardly young anymore. Even the term itself, "Christian education," is something of an embarrassment. Most major denominations no longer have agencies with the name "education" in them!

In short, we have a *vacuum in leadership* in this vital area in the life of the churches.

There was never a better time for renewal of effort, for "revival," than just now. And I am absolutely certain of these two facts:

1. A strong ministry of teaching in the churches depends on *lay* involvement, not just as participants in classes or groups but in planning and leadership as well.
2. This essential lay involvement in the church's work of teaching cannot happen without strong encouragement and support from the *clergy*.

In the last ten years I have met literally thousands of gifted laypersons in the parishes. I can say without fear of rebuttal that the most admirable work being done in the field of teaching is accomplished quietly by nonprofessional laypersons. Some of the most imaginative leadership in parish education is being provided by part-time workers who have not had formal training in the field. They began as lay volunteers, and they saturated themselves with assistance in short workshops and other events where they could learn. In time, they became real leaders in the field, often surpassing their instructors in wisdom and creativity. Public educators like to call such persons "paraprofessionals."

Lay leaders know how to support and encourage other laity.

But strong lay leadership is neither developed nor utilized where the clergy lack vision.

I am thinking of the pastors (ministers and priests) who are classified as "senior." That is to say, they are regarded by the parishioners as the chief spokespersons and most influential leaders. We go so far as to call a church "Dr. E's Church" or "Father F's Church." These men exercise incredible power and influence, and I have to say "men" because hardly any women belong to the club—yet. Senior pastors are the movers and doers in the denominations. What they want, they usually get. What they approve, they endorse. What they ignore is usually slated for neglect.

A pastor wants to be recognized as someone who is able to preach well, as one who administers programs with dispatch, as one who helps church membership to grow rather than stand still or decline, and, let's face it, as someone whose ministry produces money for church programs. These days, however, heavy involvement in Christian education doesn't loom large in the scheme. Laypersons could possibly help to change this whole picture, but they aren't alert to it.

Subtle influences come to play upon the senior pastors. I have a great deal of sympathy for these persons, for they present an interesting study: they are gifted and creative, and they have power to sway people. God needs their influence for good in the world! They work incredibly long hours and give themselves to helping people, in times of sickness, in the hour of death, and in periods of anguish and tension. They are good men, even noble.

But if someone were to say to a typical senior pastor, "Please lend your all-out support for a renewed ministry of teaching," he would probably equivocate. It just isn't the sort of cause that fits in with the image. Just think about it for a moment. Try to imagine a busy senior pastor doing any of the following things:

1. Sitting comfortably on the floor to engage in quiet conversation with a group of four-year-olds—listening more than speaking.

2. Taking a tour every Monday morning through every nook and cranny of the educational wing of the church, inspecting the closets, the bulletin board, the walls, and taking notes in order to compliment individual teachers on the evidence of attractive classroom environment. Would he shed a tear upon entering a classroom and finding everything in a shambles, with Bibles, papers, and workbooks strewn all about?

3. Going to the nearest university library to read for a day about educational issues, then leading a discussion with parish lay leaders on what he found out.

4. Reading avidly from the curricular guides for junior highs, then seeking out several boys and girls to interview with the intent of puzzling through whether the writer is speaking to their needs.

5. Telephoning the teacher of grades 5–6 to ask a specific question about how a lesson went last Sunday.

6. Learning the names and birthdays of thirty first-graders.

7. Calling up a pastor friend in another city to ask, "How did the third-graders get along in *your* church school last Sunday?"

No, we cannot imagine a typical senior pastor exhibiting such *close involvement* alongside the laity in the parish's ministry of teaching. He isn't all that interested, he isn't trained to do it, and he can't work that sort of thing into the weekly schedule.

Well, the laypersons who are the volunteers from week to week know that the clergy are not intimately interested in their work with students. For some, it does not matter; the reward is in the process and not in the degree of support they receive. For others, and especially for those who need a broader vision of the importance of volunteer teaching, the pastors' interest and support could make all the difference in the world. I am speaking about more than an occasional greeting, "How's it going?" spoken by a pastor to a lay teacher. What is needed is informed and steady support on a regular basis.

Given the present state of the churches, the really outstanding Christian education programs will not happen until the lay volunteers have this very kind of clergy support.

These same clergypersons make the key decisions on regional and national governing bodies. They decide where program emphasis is to be placed, and they determine budgets. They, too, are the decision makers who could insist on strong Christian education emphasis in the seminaries' curricula, if they wanted to take on that cause!

I am stressing both lay and clergy involvement for the improvement of teaching. Both are urgently needed, but the clergy play the crucial role. I wouldn't have thought that in an earlier period of my ministry, but I see it clearly now. It is awesome to think of the responsibility resting in the hands of pastors.

It is one thing to say these things, and quite another to come up with some practical suggestions on what to do about them. What follows is an effort in the latter direction:

1. Clergy and laity can *decide,* in a parish, that they genuinely want to work together to produce a quality program of teaching and learning. This sort of decision is not hard to work out. A task force or other core group can

be established to read, study, investigate, and make the decision: we want to have the best possible Christian education program here, and we will invest the time, effort, and money required to define what we want and to bring it to pass.

2. The focus can be placed on acquiring images of good *teaching*. The choice of materials is important but always secondary. Materials do not make the program, teachers do. Materials are the teachers' servants, not their masters. (True for public education, too.) The hardest part in the process is getting a good, clear idea of what teaching is all about.

3. Clergypersons can then help to develop, endorse, and promote good teaching through their involvements beyond the parish as well as within it. I think every association, conference, diocese, presbytery, classis, or whatever local church administrative unit you want to name, should have several people employed to travel about and help to strengthen the parish programs. Parishes are not islands to themselves; they need outside resource persons who will foster exchanges among the teachers in their areas. Clergy who sit on regional budget committees should insist on this as a priority for the health of the Christian community in these closing years of the twentieth century.

This third point will raise eyebrows, I suspect. But it is absolutely clear to me that the people in the churches would give money generously if they were sure it would really result in better teaching for children, youth, and adults. Money is available for what Christian people want, and it could be raised for the cause of Christian education. No one is asking for it, urgently, right now.

What's more, the *personnel* could be recruited. One of the tragedies of this present moment is the number of truly gifted young persons in their late teens and early twenties who cannot find jobs that challenge them, especially youth in minority groups. College graduates, honor students, have worked at minimum wage, trying hard not to be discouraged by their inability to break into the job markets.

These young persons, many of them highly idealistic and concerned about their faith as Christians, could be recruited for a *National Teachers Corps* in churches. With a few months of good training (and we do know how to provide it!), they could be employed at respectable salaries to serve as enablers, facilitators, in the parishes, working with the lay volunteers to keep the programs of teaching going from week to week.

We already have the facilities for teaching and learning. The churches are blessed with rooms, most of them empty most of the time. They could be made into scenes of joy where human beings would find their place in the heart of Christ's community, and where the reality of the Lord's presence in daily affairs would be taught and learned. How I do believe that!

To repeat, money is not the major hurdle. Great amounts are not even required. A small church with as many as three committed laypersons (with open minds and a willingness to work) could conduct a year's educational program on three hundred dollars or less. If an additional amount of two hundred dollars could go into a fund for leadership development, that would absolutely assure a good program. You will need to adjust these figures upward to allow for inflation if you read this some years from now.

The practical matters are capable of solution. The one thing no person can give to another is commitment. That has to come from inside. In the long history of the churches, commitment has emerged in times of dire need. It will again—and when it does, the "ministry of teaching" will experience renewal.

Notes

1. Augustine, *The Teacher, The Free Choice of the Will, Grace and Free Will,* tr. Robert P. Russell, *The Fathers of the Church, A New Translation,* Vol. 59 (Catholic University of America Press, 1968), pp. 8-9.

2. For a good discussion on the issues raised here, see Abraham Wandersman, Paul J. Poppen, and David F. Ricks, eds., *Humanism and Behaviorism: Dialogue and Growth* (Pergamon Press, 1976).

3. A good example is Roland S. and Doris E. Larson, *Values and Faith: Value-Clarifying Exercises for Family and Church Groups* (Winston Press, 1976).

4. An outline of James Fowler's thought is contained in the book *Life Maps* (Word Books, 1978).

5. See also Robert D. Nye, *Three Views of Man: Perspectives from Sigmund Freud, B. F. Skinner, and Carl Rogers* (Brooks/Cole Publishing Co., 1975).

6. Christians see every Biblical theme from this side of the resurrection. Any discussion of "creation," for us, assumes the presence of Christ in creation, as in John 1:1-4.

7. The equation of media and substance is intentional—the essence of all that we learn is constructed from what comes our way, from what is mediated.

8. This short, pithy essay, from which these and the following quotations are taken, is found in Alfred North Whitehead, *The Aims of Education and Other Essays* (Macmillan Co., 1929).

9. See Fynn, *Mister God, This Is Anna* (Ballantine Books, Random House, 1976).

10. Quotations that follow are from George A. Coe, *What Is Christian Education?* (Charles Scribner's Sons, 1929). See pp. 53-54.

11. See the discussion in Wayne R. Rood, *Understanding*

Christian Education (Abingdon Press, 1970), p. 189.

12. INSTROTEACH was based on IOTA (Instrument for the Observation of Teaching Activities), developed in California and expanded upon in the 1960's by Arizona State University personnel, including R. Merwin Deever, Howard J. Demeke, and Raymond E. Wochner. INSTROTEACH was published in 1968.

13. Coe, *What Is Christian Education?* p. 54.

14. See James McCosh, *The Intuitions of the Mind Inductively Investigated,* 3d ed. (Robert Carter and Brothers, 1872).

15. Carl Sagan, *The Dragons of Eden: Speculations on the Evolution of Human Intelligence* (Ballantine Books, Random House, 1977), pp. 163–195.

16. I heard Dr. Marty describe this experience in an address on "Tradition and Traditioning," at a conference sponsored by Word, Inc., in 1974.

17. See John Dewey, *Interest and Effort in Education* (Riverside Press edition, Houghton Mifflin Co., 1913; reprint ed., Southern Illinois University, 1975).

18. See *Sharing the Light of Faith: National Catechetical Directory for Catholics of the United States* (United States Catholic Conference, Department of Education, 1979).

19. One criterion I used for several years, in a church I attended, was: Could this sermon have been preached in any other century? Quite a number of them could easily have been preached in the nineteenth century, I discovered.

20. When Dr. George A. Buttrick, famed Presbyterian preacher, was entering retirement in Louisville, Kentucky, I was present on the day he spoke to the presbytery about his faith. He said that a young person had approached him on a Louisville campus to say, "Mr. Buttrick, I don't believe in preaching!" Dr. Buttrick replied, "Jerry Rubin does!" (Jerry Rubin was one of the Chicago Seven, a popular dissenter and speaker on campuses in those days.)

21. The report on the Project for the Advancement of Church Education was published under the title *The Education of Volunteers* (The Arizona Experiment, 1971).

22. I am aware that Socrates was called a midwife by Søren Kierkegaard.

23. See Jerome S. Bruner, *Toward a Theory of Instruction* (Belknap Press of Harvard University Press, 1966).

24. This juxtaposition between the words "impose" and "compose" was first called to my attention by Dr. Jeannette Veatch, professor emeritus, Arizona State University. She speaks often of

"compositive teaching" that involves students and teachers in interactive choice.

25. This episode as described in Stuart C. Henry, *George Whitefield: Wayfaring Witness* (Abingdon Press, 1957), p. 34.

26. See Dr. Evelyn Beyer, "Language Learning . . . ," *Childhood Education,* October 1971, pp. 8–11.

27. I am indebted to Dr. Buford (Gene) Wilson, of Governors State University, Illinois, for sharing insights gleaned during his study at the Center for Human Learning, University of Minnesota. He has investigated the implications of generative grammar for the design of instruction.

28. See Florence Rusterholz, " 'Miss Joy' and Memory Work to Change Lives," *Church Teachers,* Vol. 4, No. 3 (November 1976), p. 26.

29. See the following two books: Noam Chomsky, *Topics in the Theory of Generative Grammar* (The Hague: Mouton & Co., 1966), and Noam Chomsky, *Language and Responsibility: Based on Conversations with Mitsou Ronat,* tr. from the French by John Viertel (Pantheon Books, first American Edition, 1979).

30. See W. Somerset Maugham, *The Summing Up* (New American Library, A Mentor Book, 1938).

31. I got the idea of using the word "edge" from Robert M. Gagne, *The Conditions of Learning,* 2d ed. (Holt, Rinehart & Winston, 1970).

32. See, for instance, Lawrence A. Cremin, *The Wonderful World of Ellwood Patterson Cubberley: An Essay on the Historiography of American Education* (Bureau of Publications, Teachers College, Columbia University, 1965).

33. See Gabriel Moran, *Design for Religion: Toward Ecumenical Education* (Herder & Herder, 1970), pp. 146–147.

34. See especially John H. Westerhoff III, *Will Our Children Have Faith?* (Seabury Press, 1976).

35. For an excellent comparison of the Catholic and Protestant lectionaries, together with commentary, see the series of Proclamation booklets. Fortress Press is the publisher, and the series covers Cycles A, B, and C.

36. Father Alexander Schmemann teaches at St. Vladimir's Seminary, Crestwood, New York, an institution of the Orthodox Church of North America.

37. In the '50s we took great care to speak of Negroes. With the dawning of the '60s, this word was discarded in favor of "Black is beautiful."

38. During the years 1974–1977, the National Teacher Educa-

tion Project (NTEP) conducted courses in learning laboratories at Presbyterian School of Christian Education, Richmond, Virginia, and at Louisville Presbyterian Theological Seminary, Louisville, Kentucky. These laboratories were funded by Lilly Endowment, Inc., Indianapolis. At the end of the three-year period, they were closed because of heavy financial deficits for their operation. (The laboratory equipment in Richmond was purchased by the school, and the courses were incorporated into the regular curriculum.) I served as an adjunct professor at both of these institutions.

39. I look upon these pressing issues in Roman Catholicism as interrelated: the role of women; celibacy of the clergy; abortion and right-to-life; birth control by artificial contraception. All belong under the heading "human sexuality," and they are certain to be studied carefully for years to come.

40. There is great need for a "thesaurus" of Christian education that will identify concepts currently being taught and indicate where to find relevant data in curricular publications.